INLG 2017 Workshop on Computational Creativity in Natural Language Generation (CC-NLG 2017)

Santiago de Compostela, Spain
4 September 2017

ISBN: 978-1-5108-4760-6

Printed from e-media with permission by:

Curran Associates, Inc.
57 Morehouse Lane
Red Hook, NY 12571

CURRAN ASSOCIATES INC. proceedings.com

Some format issues inherent in the e-media version may also appear in this print version.

Printed by Curran Associates, Inc. (2017)

Association for Computational Linguistics
209 N. Eighth Street
Stroudsburg, Pennsylvania 18360

Phone: 1-570-476-8006
Fax: 1-570-476-0860

acl@aclweb.org

Additional copies of this publication are available from:

Curran Associates, Inc.
57 Morehouse Lane
Red Hook, NY 12571 USA
Phone: 845-758-0400
Fax: 845-758-2633
Email: curran@proceedings.com
Web: www.proceedings.com

The INLG 2017 Workshop on

Computational Creativity in Natural Language Generation

Proceedings of the Workshop

4th September 2017
University of Santiago Compostela
Spain

Introduction

Welcome to the second edition of the Workshop on Computational Creativity in Natural Language Generation (CC-NLG), collocated with INLG 2017, the International Conference on Natural Language Generation. As a follow-up of CC-NLG 2016, this workshop builds upon the dynamic of bringing together researchers dealing with text generation from a computational creativity perspective, and researchers in natural language generation with an interest in creative aspects.

These two communities have been working separately for many years, as the focus in each one of them has been different: creativity research tends to be less focused on technical issues in natural language generation, and more on issues related to cognition, aesthetics, and novelty; while NLG research tends to focus on technical and theoretical aspects of processes, the informativeness of textual content, and readability of output. However, recent progress in both fields is reducing many of these differences – with creativity projects moving more towards robust implementation, and NLG research including stylistics, variation and literary genres such as poetry or narrative. We believe they are now approaching the point where they can mutually benefit from ongoing work. By encouraging members of both communities to discuss work in related topics with each other, we hope to move towards better joint understanding of the problems involved.

These proceedings include a total of five papers, three focused on poetry generation and two on story generation.

Hugo Gonçalo Oliveira, Ben Burtenshaw, Mike Kestemont, Tom De Smedt

Organizers

Workshop Chairs:

Hugo Gonçalo Oliveira, University of Coimbra
Ben Burtenshaw, University of Antwerp
Mike Kestemont, University of Antwerp
Tom De Smedt, University of Antwerp

Program Committee:

Pablo Gervás, Universidad Complutense de Madrid
Matthew Purver, Queen Mary University of London
Ehud Reiter, University of Aberdeen
Cyril Labbé, Université Grenoble Alpe
François Portet, Université Grenoble Alpes
Hannu Toivonen, University of Helsinki
Alessandro Valitutti, University College Dublin
Tony Veale, University College Dublin
Rafael Pérez y Pérez, Universidad Autónoma Metropolitana at Cuajimalpa
Raquel Hervás, Universidad Complutense de Madrid
Amílcar Cardoso, University of Coimbra
Carlos León, Universidad Complutense de Madrid
Sascha Griffiths, Universität Hamburg
Folgert Karsdorp, Meertens Instituut, Royal Dutch Academy of Arts and Sciences
Florian Kunneman, Radboud University, Nijmegen

Table of Contents

Conference Programme

Monday, 4th September

	14:30–16:30 Session 1
14:30–14:40	Short introduction
14:40–15:30	*A Feast for the Senses in 140 Characters or Less* (Invited Talk) Tony Veale
15:30–16:00	*O Poeta Artificial 2.0: Increasing Meaningfulness in a Poetry Generation Twitter bot* Hugo Gonçalo Oliveira
16:00–16:30	*Template-Free Construction of Poems with Thematic Cohesion and Enjambment* Pablo Gervás
16:30–17:00	Coffee break
	17:00–19:00 Session 2
17:00–17:30	*Poet's Little Helper: A methodology for computer-based poetry generation. A case study for the Basque language* Aitzol Astigarraga, José María Martínez-Otzeta, Igor Rodriguez, Basilio Sierra and Elena Lazkano
17:30–17:50	*If then or else: Who for whom about what in which* Manuel Portela and Ana Marques Da Silva
17:50–18:10	*Constructing narrative using a generative model and continuous action policies* Emmanouil Theofanis Chourdakis and Joshua Reiss
18:10–18:40	*Synthetic Literature: Writing Science Fiction in a Co-Creative Process* Enrique Manjavacas, Folgert Karsdorp, Ben Burtenshaw and Mike Kestemont
18:40	Close

Invited Talk

A Feast for the Senses in 140 Characters or Less
Making Generation More Personal, Affective and Perceptually Grounded

By Tony Veale, School of Computer Science, University College Dublin, Ireland.

Shakespeare wrote that a rose by any other name would smell just as sweet, but would this alternate name be just as effective as a metaphor? Perhaps, though any figurative uses would surely depend on the exact makeup of the new name. Were we to instead refer to a rose as a "goreweed," a "prickbleed," a "bloodwort" or a "turdblossom" we would surely have to find new metaphorical uses for this familiar flower. Our metaphors do more than evoke lexical semantics in the mind of a reader, and the very best can tap into our memories and perceptual faculties to create a feast for the senses, one that is as rich in colour, texture and aroma as it is in semantic meaning. So when we bend our machines to the interpretation and generation of novel metaphors, we must ensure they are as adept with the multi-modal connotations of words as they are with their denotative semantics. In this work I explore the mutual grounding of linguistic metaphors in non-linguistic multi-modal stimuli – such as colours and abstract generative art – and vice versa: I show how non-representational visual stimuli can serve to bind together the various elements of a complex linguistic metaphor, to squeeze more meaning and connotation from the words than an utterance alone can manage. In each case these elements are further grounded in the social and the personal, insofar as the machine-crafted metaphors are generated to reflect the real-time behavioral traits of real people – the metaphor's intended audience – on social media. I demonstrate the various strands of this work using real Twitter "bots" such as @MetaphorMagnet, @BestOfBotWorlds and @BotOnBotAction. These bots are autonomous AI systems that are designed to interact with real people on Twitter and to showcase the applicability of machine-generated (but human-targeted and human-centered) metaphors in social media. I aim to show how they can offer an ideal vehicle for exploring the related themes of symbolic grounding, affective meaning and multi-modal creativity in language generation.

Poet's Little Helper: A methodology for computer-based poetry generation. A case study for the Basque language

Aitzol Astigarraga and **José María Martínez-Otzeta**
and **Igor Rodriguez** and **Basilio Sierra** and **Elena Lazkano**
Department of Computer Science and Artificial Intelligence
University of the Basque Country UPV/EHU
Donostia-San Sebastian 20018, Spain
aitzol.astigarraga@ehu.eus

Abstract

We present Poet's Little Helper (PLH), a tool that implements a methodology to generate poetry using minimal language-dependent information. The user only needs to provide a corpus with a set of sentences, a rhyme checker and a syllable-counter. From these building blocks, PLH produces: (1) an exploratory analysis of the suitability of the given corpus for poetry generation. (2) a novel and non-trivial poem grammatically correct under metrical and rhyming constraints. This poem also shows content that is coherent with a topic given by the user. The process of poetry generation is a cycle with three phases: lexical exploratory analysis, semantic exploratory analysis and poem generation. The goal is twofold: on the one hand PLH aims to be a useful open source poem-generator for many languages with minimal effort; on the other hand, analizes how the particularities of each corpus affect in the creation of poems. The presented PHL tool is offered in a public repository. The results of an experiment with a corpus of Basque texts is shown.

1 Introduction

Poetry is a form of literary expression intended to convey emotions in the audience, and in which the expression of feelings and ideas is given intensity by the use of style and rhythm according to predefined formal rules. Poetry generation is a challenging field in the area of Natural Language Processing. When a poem is automatically created by computational means, usually the programmer takes advantage of existing general semantic knowledge from resources like WordNet for semantic validation, or of already known formalized grammars for sentence generation. Furthermore, most of the existing poetry-generation systems are devoted to the English language (Gonçalo Oliveira, 2015). For minority languages with low presence in the natural language processing community the most usual scenario is a lack of such computational resources.

In this paper we present a methodology to help researchers in generating poetry automatically. This methodology is composed of two different phases: the first one devoted to the exploratory analysis (lexical and semantic) of the corpora provided for poetry generation, and the second one focused on the automatic generation of the final poem given the results of the previous phase. We provide a tool which implements the above mentioned steps.

The rest of the paper is organized as follows: section 2 introduces the main poetry generation systems and the strategy implemented in the PLH tool; section 3 aims to give a formal definition of the presented methodology; section 4 describes the source code of the PLH tool; section 5 shows an application of the proposed method to the Basque language; and the final section 6 presents the conclusions and possible future lines of research.

2 Poetry Generation

Computational modeling for poetry generation has become a topic in the artificial intelligence community in recent years. Before the computer science community took an interest in the area, people with a background closer to humanities made early efforts in systematic generation of poetry. We could

Proceedings of the INLG 2017 Workshop on Computational Creativity and Natural Language Generation, pages 2–10,
Santiago de Compostela, September 2017.

mention works related to generating variations over a predetermined set of verses (Queneau, 1961), or to select a template to produce poems from it (Oulipo, 1981).

In recent years many different computer-based poetry generation systems have been developed. Among the most relevant ones we could include the well-known WASP (Gervás, 2000; Gervás, 2010), a Spanish verse-generation system developed following the generate-and-test strategy; Full-FACE (Colton et al., 2012), a corpus-based poetry generation system which introduces emotions in the generation process; PoeTryMe (Gonçalo Oliveira et al., 2014; Gonçalo Oliveira and Cardoso, 2015), a poetry generation platform used for Portuguese, Spanish and English; DopeLearning (Malmi et al., 2016), where the task of lyric generation is formulated as an information retrieval task. An approach using text mining methods, morphological analysis, and morphological synthesis to produce poetry in Finnish is presented in (Toivanen et al., 2012). Constraint programming for poetry composition is explored in (Toivanen et al., 2013). In (Agirrezabal et al., 2013) an approach of poetry generation based on POS-tag is described. Markov chains are also widely used as a basis of poetry generation systems. Popular and recent examples of N-gram generators are (Barbieri et al., 2012; Das and Gambäck, 2014; Gervás, 2016).

For a more thorough review of systems related to automatic generation of poetry, we point the reader to (Gervás, 2013) and (Lamb et al., 2016).

Our poetry generator is based on the following principles:

- Form: rhyme and metric compound the technical requirements of a verse. Thus, finding rhymes and counting syllables are essential abilities that the system must perform.
- Content: the output of the verse generator module must be meaningful. Methods to measure the semantic coherence of the generated text are needed.

The verse generation procedure relies in the extraction of sentences from corpora and combining them (under rhyme and metric constraints) to form the final poem. Semantic relatedness or internal coherence between poem verses is measured with an implementation of LSA (Latent Semantic Analysis) method (Deerwester et al., 1990). The main assumption of LSA is that words that are close in meaning will occur in similar pieces of text. A matrix containing word counts per verse is constructed from a corpus and singular value decomposition (SVD) is used to reduce the dimensionality of the semantic space. Verses are then compared by taking the cosine distance between their two vector representations, where a higher value is associated with a higher semantic similarity.

Thus, in a basic scenario, the user provides a topic and the kind of poem to be composed, and the system aims to give as output a novel poem with content semantically related to the proposed topic.

3 Methodology

In this section the proposed methodology is described. The process of poetry generation is a cycle with three phases: lexical exploratory analysis, semantic exploratory analysis and poem generation. Lexical and semantic richness is largely required for acceptable poem generation, and exploring the lexical and semantic dimensions of the data could help the researcher to focus on improving it along their weaknesses.

3.1 Lexical exploratory analysis

Regarding the lexical exploratory analysis, we define the following actions:

- *Count the number of potential verses.*
- *Find the number of verses which do not adjust to the rhyming convention, and show their endings.*
- *Find the number of verses which rhyme with a given word, and list them.*
- *Compute the number of rhyming equivalence classes of the set of verses.* A rhyming equivalence class is a set of verses which share the same rhyming pattern.
- *Compute the number of rhyming equivalence classes of the set of verses that have more elements than the minimum number of rhyming verses in a poem.* This is the number of valid

Proceedings of the INLG 2017 Workshop on Computational Creativity and Natural Language Generation, pages 2–10,
Santiago de Compostela, September 2017. ©2017 Association for Computational Linguistics

equivalence classes, in the sense that elements from the other equivalence classes cannot form part of a poem.

- *Create a list with a verse from every equivalence class along with the number of elements in such equivalence class.*
- *Plot the number of verses in each equivalence class.*
- *Plot the logarithm of the number of verses in each equivalence class.* Useful when the distribution is very skewed.
- *Plot the histogram of the number of equivalence classes according to the equivalence class size.* Another way of exploring the distribution of equivalence classes according to their size.
- *Plot the histogram of the number of equivalence classes according to the logarithm of the equivalence class size.*

3.2 Semantic analysis

The semantic exploratory analysis subtask is comprised of several steps:

- *Build a semantic model from the set of documents Ds provided by the user.*
- *Find the verses more similar to a given theme according to the semantic models.*
- *Find the verses more similar to a given theme according to the semantic models and that also rhyme with a sentence.*

3.3 Poetry generation

For the poetry generation subtask the steps are the following:

- *Ignore equivalence classes with fewer elements that the minimum needed.* In this step the equivalence classes from which a poem cannot be created are ignored.
- *Compute the best poems given a theme according to a goodness function.* Several goodness functions are available to create poems.

3.4 Formal definition

Let us start with some terminology. $\mathbb{N}$ will denote the set of natural numbers. $\mathbb{R}$ will denote the set of real numbers. A document $d \in D$ is a sequence of words ($w \in W$) and punctuation marks ($m \in M$) and spaces which follows the syntactic conventions of the language. A verse $v \in V$ is a document d under some restrictions. The power set of a set S will be denoted with $\mathcal{P}(S)$.

The elements that the user has to define before applying this methodology are the following:

- *A set of documents (Ds) which is used to infer the semantic models used later.*
- *A set of documents (Dv) which is used to obtain the verses.*
- *A set of (M) of punctuation marks.* The elements of this set will be removed when performing semantic analysis.
- *A natural number $NV \in \mathbb{N}_{\neq 0}$ denoting the number of verses in a poem.*
- *A sequence of rhyme patterns $RP \in \{0, 1, ..., NV\}^{NV}$.* The rhyme patterns in the poem have to be encoded in the following manner: the rhyme pattern of the first verse corresponds to the number zero; for the pattern of a new verse, if such a rhyming pattern already exists, the number corresponding to that pattern is written, or the first natural number not yet chosen otherwise. For example, four verses with the same rhyming pattern would be written as 0, 0, 0, 0. Six verses with rhyming patterns by consecutive pairs will be 0, 0, 1, 1, 2, 2. The pattern 0, 1, 1, 2, 2, 1, 1, 0 would corresponding to eight verses where the last three patterns are the same as the first three patterns, but reversed.
- *A function ($extract\_verses : D \to \mathcal{P}(V)$) that extracts all the potential verses from a document.*
- *A lemmatizer function ($lemmatize : W \to W$), which returns a lemmatized word.*

Proceedings of the INLG 2017 Workshop on Computational Creativity and Natural Language Generation, pages 2–10,
Santiago de Compostela, September 2017. ©2017 Association for Computational Linguistics

- *A rhyming function ($is\_rhyme : D^2 \rightarrow \{T, F\}$) that returns True if the two documents rhyme, and False otherwise.*

The system should already have other elements defined. In the following functions, $\mathbb{S}$ will denote the set of semantic models.

- *A function ($clean\_document : D \times M \rightarrow D$) which returns the document without punctuation marks.*

- *A function ($semantics\_extractor : D \times \mathbb{N} \times W^* \times \mathbb{N} \times \mathbb{R} \rightarrow \mathbb{S}$) that returns a semantic model.* This function takes five parameters to generate a semantic model (LSA). The parameters are: a set of documents used to build the semantic model; the number of topics which should be used to create the semantic model; a list of words to be removed from the documents; a parameter indicating the minimum document number in which a word should appear; and a parameter indicating the maximum fraction of the total documents in which a word could appear.

- *A similarity function ($sim : D^2 \rightarrow R$), which returns the similarity between two documents.*

- *A rhyme detector function ($rhyme\_generator : D \times \mathcal{P}(V) \rightarrow \mathcal{P}(V)$), which returns all the rhyming verses given a document.*

- *Several poem generator functions ($poem\_generator : V \times D \times \mathbb{N} \times \mathbb{N}^{NV} \times \mathbb{S} \rightarrow \mathcal{P}(V)$), that given a set of verses, a document, a number of verses, a rhyming pattern and a semantic model, returns a poem under the constraints imposed by the number of verses and the rhyming pattern; the poem will be semantically related to a document under a semantic model.* The document above referred can be viewed as the theme of the poem. These generator functions will differ in their inner implementation of another two auxiliary functions: a poem validator function ($poem\_validator : \mathcal{P}(V) \rightarrow \{T, F\}$), which returns True if the poem conforms to the poetry rules, and False otherwise, and a poem goodness function ($poem\_goodness : \mathcal{P}(V) \rightarrow \mathbb{R}$), which returns a value for every set of verses according to its quality.

4 Open source code

A public repository has been created with the basic code needed to implement this methodology [1]. The code is a collection of Python modules and Jupyter notebooks, which, after installation, allows people with little knowledge of the Python language to perform the analysis on their own.

The structure of the code is the following:

4.1 Modules

- *Customize.* It contains the following definitions, that have to be customized according to the needs of the researcher: the filenames where D_s and D_v are stored, M and *RP* as Python tuples, the natural number *NV*, and the functions *extract_verses*, *lemmatize* and *is_rhyme*.

- *General.* General functions not directly related to natural language processing or poetry generation. For instance, list manipulation or histogram drawing functions are defined here.

- *NLP.* Functions related to natural language processing. The construction and manipulation of semantic models takes place here.

- *Poetry.* Functions related to poetry generation. Rhyming and poem construction takes place here.

4.2 Notebooks

- *Get_started.* This notebook will be called from the other two. The researcher does not need to open it, given that it only contains some code that is automatically executed to initialize the system.

- *Exploratory_analysis.* Here, the code that allows exploration of the lexical and semantic possibilities of the verses is located.

[1] https://github.com/rsait/PLH

Proceedings of the INLG 2017 Workshop on Computational Creativity and Natural Language Generation, pages 2–10,
Santiago de Compostela, September 2017.

- *poem_generation.* The notebook where the last step, the poetry generation, is performed. The researcher, after analyzing the data with the *Exploratory_analysis* notebook, is ready to execute this code and create automated poetry.

5 Case study

Verse improvisation (under the name of *Bertsolaritza*) is a traditional cultural expression in the Basque Country. With ancient roots, it has undergone a revival in the last times, being widely popular.

In this section we present the experiments made with a corpus of Basque texts to produce poems under the formal requirements of Basque poetry. This corpus is the set of all the news that appeared in the Basque newspaper Egunkaria in the years 2002-2003, which comprises 1,277,457 sentences. The results of the exploratory analysis are shown along with some automatically produced poetry. The selected poetry meter for experiments is *Zortziko Txikia*, a composition of eight lines in which odd lines have seven syllables and even ones have six. The union of each odd line with the next even line, forms a verse. Each verse has 13 syllables with a caesura after the 7th syllable (7 + 6) and must rhyme with the others[2].

5.1 Building blocks

As previously said, some building blocks are needed in order to apply the proposed methodology. In this case those blocks were defined in the following manner:

- The set of documents Ds from which the semantics models are created is the Basque corpus previously referenced.
- The set of documents Dv from which extract the potential verses is equivalent to Ds.
- The set of punctuation marks is M = (, . ? ! " ' / \).
- A $syllable\_counter$ function that counts the syllables of the input text.
- The rhyming function is_rhyme that returns all the rhyming lines given an input line. It is based on (Amuriza, 1981) and implemented using regular expressions.
- The natural number NV that denotes the number of verses in a poem. In *Zortziko Txikia* this number is 4.
- The sequence of rhyme patterns RP. In *Zortziko Txikia* this sequence is (0, 0, 0, 0). It means that all the verses have to rhyme among themselves.

5.2 Lexical exploratory analysis

The following actions have been performed automatically with the help of our lexical exploratory software:

- Count the number of potential verses: 41659.
- Find the number of verses which do not adjust to the Basque rhyming conventions: 139. Percentage of the total: 0.33%.
- Find the last words of such verses. Analyzing these words we find the sign %, making us wonder if we should expand the set M, filter these kind of characters or make another decision. We also find interjections ("eh", "hi"), foreign proper names ("olaf", "jerusalem", "bush"), Basque proper names ("unanue", "orue"), Roman numerals ("xix", "xx", "xxi"), acronyms ("eajk", "ugt", "upn") and other words not easily classifiable. After these step we could decide what to do in every case: for example, we could modify the rhyming function to add those Basque names, expand acronyms or Roman numerals in the original documents and repeat the verse extraction process, or remove all the no rhyming verses. We have chosen this last option, that is provided by our software.
- Compute the number of equivalence classes of the set of verses, according to the rhyme. In this example the number of partitions is 184.
- Compute the number of equivalence classes of the set of verses that have more elements than

[2] http://www.bertsozale.eus/en/bertsolaritza/what-is-a-bertso

Proceedings of the INLG 2017 Workshop on Computational Creativity and Natural Language Generation, pages 2–10,
Santiago de Compostela, September 2017.

the minimum number of rhyming verses in a poem. In Zortziko Txikia the rhyme pattern (RP) is (0, 0, 0, 0), which means any valid partition has to contain at least four elements, because a poem is composed by four rhyming verses. The number of equivalence classes of minimum size in our example is 141. If RP would be (0, 1, 0, 1, 0, 1), the minimum equivalence class size would be three, and in the case of (0, 1, 0, 1, 2, 2), the minimum size would be two.

- Create a list with a verse of every equivalence class along with the number of elements in such equivalence class. Our list is of the form [('a aita zenarekin joan zen bertara', 4441), ('a arrieta hartu zituzten mendean', 4209), ... , ('zeelandarrekin ez da ariko lomu', 1), ('ziganda badiola zalakain gaztelu', 1)].

- Plot the number of verses in each equivalence class (figure 1), the logarithm of the number of verses in each equivalence class (figure 2), the histogram of the number of equivalence classes according to the equivalence class size (figure 3) and the histogram of the number of equivalence classes according to the logarithm of the equivalence class size (figure 4).

These four figures can help the user in the interpretation of the distribution of the rhyming equivalence classes and their relative size, that appears to follow a power law (Piantadosi, 2014).

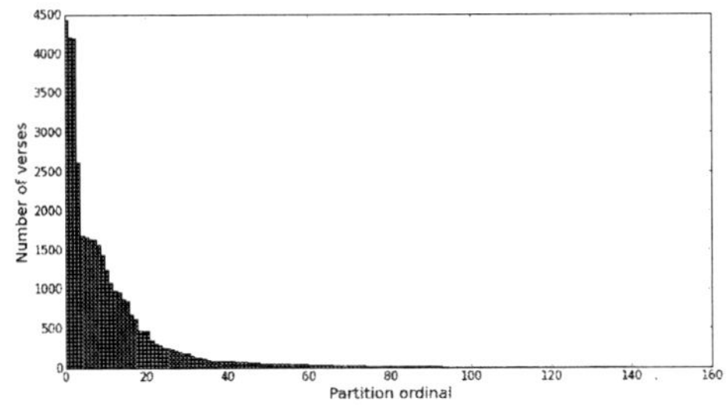

Figure 1: Number of verses in each equivalence class

5.3 Semantic exploratory analysis

The following actions have been performed automatically with the help of our semantic exploratory software:

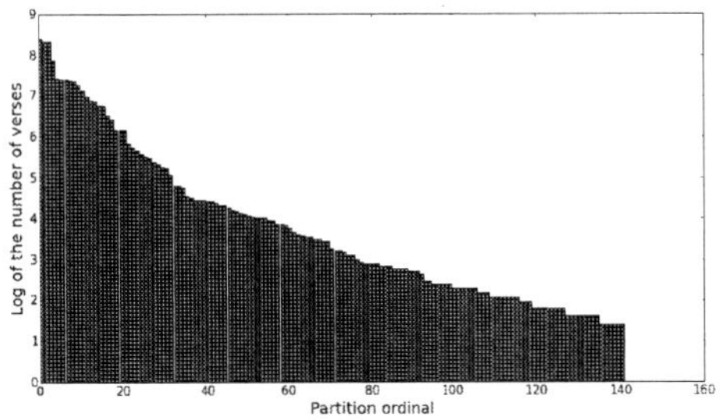

Figure 2: Logarithm of the number of verses in each equivalence class

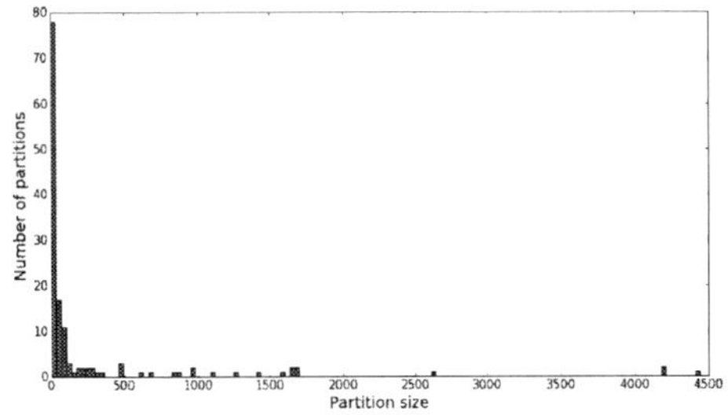

Figure 3: Histogram of the number of equivalence classes according to the equivalence class size

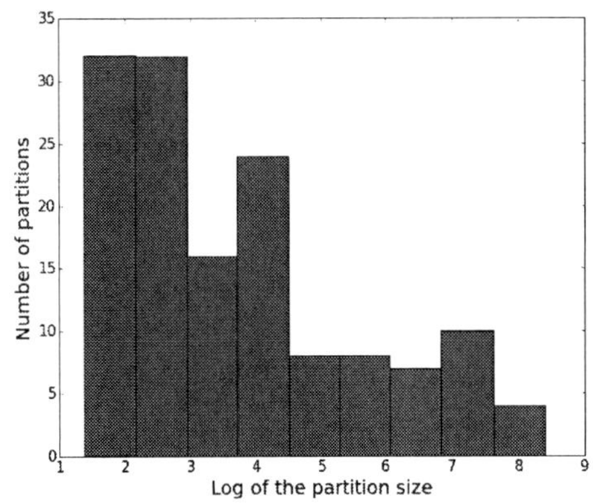

Figure 4: Histogram of the number of equivalence class according to the logarithm of the equivalence class size

- Build a semantic model from the set of documents Ds provided by the user. The number of topics has been assigned to 100, filtering all the words that do not appear in at least 5 documents, and all the words that appear in more than 20% of the documents. We have also filtered the stopwords.

- Find the verses more similar to a given theme according to the semantic models. Taking for example the theme "itsaso" (sea), we find sen-

Proceedings of the INLG 2017 Workshop on Computational Creativity and Natural Language Generation, pages 2–10, Santiago de Compostela, September 2017. ©2017 Association for Computational Linguistics

tences with the word "itsaso", but also sentences without that word, but other related words, as "txalupa" (small boat) or "ur" (water). We find sentences with the word "ontzi", that could be translated as "ship" but also as a "generic container", highlighting the challenging issues which polysemy implies.

- Find the verses which are more similar to a given theme according to the semantic models and that also rhyme with a sentence. Following with the "itsaso" example, the more similar verse is 'oliobideetan eta itsasoan', with a similarity value of 0.99833471). The three sentences more similar to "itsaso" that also fulfil the rhyming restrictions, along with their similarity values, are ('zenbait otzara eta ontzi hareatzan', 0.91221404), ('paper eta ontzien birziklapenean', 0.88736451), and ('delas eta izura oraindik ontzian', 0.83049005).

5.4 Poetry generation

For a poem to be valid, it has to be composed of the number of verses given by *NV* and follow the rhyming pattern given by *RP*. No two verses are allowed to share the same final word. In the following we will refer to the document to which the poem has to be semantically related, as the theme t. Two different *poem_generator* strategies have been used to build a poem.

1. Choose the verse v more similar to the theme t. Then choose the $NV-1$ verses more similar to t that follow the rhyming pattern RP.

2. Choose the ten verses v more similar to the theme t. Then, for each of the ten verses, choose the $NV-1$ verses more similar to t that follow the rhyming pattern RP. The poem with highest score is chosen.

For each of these two functions, two examples are shown, using different themes t. In the first example, the theme "itsaso" (sea) has been chosen, and in the other "gurasoak" (parents) has been used. NV is equal to four, and the RP pattern is (0, 0, 0, 0), meaning that all the verses have to share the same rhyming pattern.

The verse more similar to the theme is 'oliobideetan eta itsasoan' (in oil paths and in the sea). The poem generated choosing the three verses more similar to to theme is shown in Table 1.

Table 1: Poem created with the verse more similar to the theme "itsaso" ("sea") (in Basque and its English translation)

Basque	oliobideetan eta itsasoan atentatu susmoak itsaso beltzean itsaso baretura itzuli nahian zenbait otzara eta ontzi hareatzan
English	in oil paths and in the sea attack rumors in the sea's darkness trying to return to calm sea several container and ships are going on

The same experiment has been performed choosing the best ten verses and then computing the best poem among the ten ones generated. The same poem is ranked the first with this approach, but in our opinion, the poem in Table 2 (which ranked 8th of 10) is the best of all ten.

Table 2: Best poem in our opinion with the theme "itsaso" ("sea") (in Basque and its English translation)

Basque	Kantauri itsasoa haserre zeharo ozeano haunditan egin dugu txango putz egitea ere tokatu ezkero maitatu eta negar egin baitut Bilbo
English	Cantabrian Sea very angry we have made a trip to the vast stormy ocean if we are emerged to make blow I have loved and cried, Bilbao

Table 3: Poem created with the verse more similar to the theme "gurasoak" ("parents") (in Basque and its English translation)

Basque	nire gurasoentzat Peret kristona zen haiekin bi urteko alaba zeukaten familia osoak topa zitezkeen noizbait haur bat badator nahiz ez jakin nor den
English	Peret was very good in my parents' opinion with these people they had a two years old daughter for all the family to get together sometimes a child comes and I do not know who (s)he is

In the second example the theme "gurasoak" ("parents") has been chosen. With the same procedure as in the first example, the verse more similar to the theme is 'nire gurasoentzat Peret kristona zen' (Peret[3] was very good in my parents' opinion), and the poem generated choosing the three verses more similar to the theme is shown in Table 3. When performing the same experiment with the best ten verses, another poem, shown in Table 4 is chosen. As in the previous example, we found the poem in Table 5 (ranked 10th of 10) the best for our liking.

[3] A Spanish singer

Proceedings of the INLG 2017 Workshop on Computational Creativity and Natural Language Generation, pages 2–10,
Santiago de Compostela, September 2017.

Table 4: Best poem built from the ten verses more similar to the theme "gurasoak" ("parents") (in Basque and its English translation)

Basque	ikastolako haurren txanda izango da haurtzaindegietatik haur eskoletara haur danborradarako Easo Ederra eta gero eta haur gehiago dira
English	It will be school children turn from nursery to school children drum performance in San Sebastian there are more and more kids

Table 5: Best poem in our opinion with the theme "gurasoak" ("parents") (in Basque and its English translation)

Basque	ahizpa ere haurrei irakasten dabil aitona hola dabil makur eta ixil zuk errondak atera bai ibili trankil Londreseko Paddington geltokitik hurbil
English	(S)he is teaching to his/her sister and children the grandfather goes on bowed and silent you carry on calm proposing challenges close to London's Paddington station

Let us remember that the goal of the methodology and the associated code is to help the user to explore the possibilities of their data. In this example we find that the generated poems are not of high quality, and that even we do not agree with the relative ordering of them given by the code. So, which conclusions could we extract from these facts? We already have tools to find all the verses related to a theme ordered by relevance, so one first step could be to check if such ordering is suitable. If that it is not the case, it is very likely the process of the semantic model construction needs some tuning. Or maybe the problem lies in the few number of verses that rhyme with the most promising candidates. This could be also explored with our tool. In our case, it looks as if the verses with a haiku-like structure are better valued by our ear. This makes us wonder if the poem goodness function could take into account this fact, and weight down the poems with all the verses very related to the theme, or those with too many repeated words between verses.

6 Conclusions and further work

In this work a methodology to guide the exploration of the possibilities of a collection of documents to perform automatic poetry generation has been described. Along with it a tool and its source code written in Python has been presented. The possibilities of the system have been shown with an example in Basque language.

As further work, we intend to add more functionalities to the lexical and semantic exploratory subsystems, as well as to the poetry generation subsystem. Another ways of building poems, as for example using genetic algorithms or Markov chains, would be of interest. The *poem_goodness* functions are fixed and predefined, but it would be possible to be customizable by the researcher. Another idea would be to get a feedback from the researcher or a knowledgeable user about the subjective goodness of a poem, in order to improve the goodness functions that the system uses. At this moment a brute force approach is applied in the lexical and semantic exploration and in the poetry generation, which could imply a heavy computational load with big corpora. We plan to tackle these issues in new versions of the software.

Acknowledgements

This paper has been supported by the Spanish Ministerio de Economía y Competitividad, contract TIN2015-64395-R (MINECO/FEDER, UE), as well as by the Basque Government, contract IT900-16.

References

Manex Agirrezabal, Bertol Arrieta, Aitzol Astigarraga, and Mans Hulden. 2013. POS-Tag based poetry generation with WordNet. In *ENLG 2013 - Proceedings of the 14th European Workshop on Natural Language Generation, August 8-9, 2013, Sofia, Bulgaria*, pages 162–166.

Xabier Amuriza. 1981. *Hiztegi Errimatua (Rhyming Dictionary)*. Lanku Kultur Zerbitzuak (publisher).

Gabriele Barbieri, François Pachet, Pierre Roy, and Mirko Degli Esposti. 2012. Markov constraints for generating lyrics with style. In *Proceedings of the 20th European Conference on Artificial Intelligence*, pages 115–120. IOS Press.

Simon Colton, Jacob Goodwin, and Tony Veale. 2012. Full-FACE poetry generation. In *Proceedings of the Third International Conference on Computational Creativity*, pages 95–102.

Amitava Das and Björn Gambäck. 2014. Poetic machine: Computational creativity for automatic poetry generation in bengali. In *5th International Conference on Computational Creativity, ICCC*, pages 230–238.

Scott Deerwester, Susan T Dumais, George W Furnas, Thomas K Landauer, and Richard Harshman. 1990.

Proceedings of the INLG 2017 Workshop on Computational Creativity and Natural Language Generation, pages 2–10,
Santiago de Compostela, September 2017.

Indexing by latent semantic analysis. *Journal of the American society for information science*, 41(6):391–407.

Pablo Gervás. 2000. WASP: Evaluation of different strategies for the automatic generation of Spanish verse. In *Proceedings of the AISB-00 Symposium on Creative & Cultural Aspects of AI*, pages 93–100. Citeseer.

Pablo Gervás. 2010. Engineering linguistic creativity: Bird flight and jet planes. In *Proceedings of the NAACL HLT 2010 Second Workshop on Computational Approaches to Linguistic Creativity*, pages 23–30. Association for Computational Linguistics.

Pablo Gervás. 2013. Computational modelling of poetry generation. In *Artificial Intelligence and Poetry Symposium, AISB Convention 2013*, University of Exeter, United Kingdom. The Society for the Study of Artificial Intelligence and the Simulation of Behaviour.

Pablo Gervás. 2016. Constrained creation of poetic forms during theme-driven exploration of a domain defined by an N-gram model. *Connection Science*, 28(2):111–130.

Hugo Gonçalo Oliveira and Amílcar Cardoso. 2015. Poetry generation with PoeTryMe. In *Computational Creativity Research: Towards Creative Machines*, pages 243–266. Springer.

Hugo Gonçalo Oliveira, Raquel Hervás, Alberto Díaz, and Pablo Gervás. 2014. Adapting a generic platform for poetry generation to produce spanish poems. In *ICCC*, pages 63–71.

Hugo Gonçalo Oliveira. 2015. Automatic generation of poetry inspired by twitter trends. In *International Joint Conference on Knowledge Discovery, Knowledge Engineering, and Knowledge Management*, pages 13–27. Springer.

Carolyn Lamb, Daniel G Brown, and Charles LA Clarke. 2016. A taxonomy of generative poetry techniques. In *Bridges Finland Conference Proceedings*, pages 195–202.

E. Malmi, P. Takala, H. Toivonen, T. Raiko, and A. Gionis. 2016. Dopelearning: a computational approach to rap lyrics generation. In *Proceedings of the 22nd ACM SIGKDD International Conference on Knowledge Discovery and Data Mining*, pages 195–204.

Association Oulipo. 1981. *Atlas de litterature potentielle*. Collection Idees. Gallimard.

Steven T Piantadosi. 2014. Zipf's word frequency law in natural language: A critical review and future directions. *Psychonomic bulletin & review*, 21(5):1112–1130.

Raymond Queneau. 1961. *100.000.000.000.000 de poemes*. Gallimard Series. Schoenhof's Foreign Books.

Jukka Toivanen, Hannu Toivonen, Alessandro Valitutti, Oskar Gross, et al. 2012. Corpus-based generation of content and form in poetry. In *Proceedings of the Third International Conference on Computational Creativity*, pages 175–179.

Jukka Toivanen, Matti Järvisalo, Hannu Toivonen, et al. 2013. Harnessing constraint programming for poetry composition. In *Proceedings of the Fourth International Conference on Computational Creativity*, pages 160–167.

Proceedings of the INLG 2017 Workshop on Computational Creativity and Natural Language Generation, pages 2–10,
Santiago de Compostela, September 2017.

O Poeta Artificial 2.0: Increasing Meaningfulness in a Poetry Generation Twitter bot

Hugo Gonçalo Oliveira
CISUC, Department of Informatics Engineering
University of Coimbra, Portugal
hroliv@dei.uc.pt

Abstract

O Poeta Artificial is a bot that tweets poems, in Portuguese, inspired by the latest Twitter trends. Built on top of PoeTryMe, a poetry generation platform, so far it had only produced poems based on a set of keywords in tweets about a trend. This paper presents recently implemented features for increasing the connection between the produced text and the target trend through the reutilisation and production of new text fragments, for highlighting the trend, paraphrasing text by Twitter users, or based on extracted or inferred semantic relations.

1 Introduction

Poetry generation is a popular task at the intersection of Computational Creativity and Natural Language Generation. It aims at producing text that exhibits poetic features at formal and content level, while, to some extent, syntactic rules should still be followed and a meaningful message should be transmitted, often through figurative language. Instead of generating a poem that uses a set of user-given keywords or around an abstract concept, several poetry generators produce poetry inspired by a given prose document. Besides the potential application to entertainment, this provides a specific and tighter context for assessing the poem's interpretability.

This paper presents new features of *O Poeta Artificial* (Portuguese for "The Artificial Poet"), a computational system that produces poems written in Portuguese, inspired by the latest trends on the social network Twitter and, similarly to other creative systems, posts them in the same network, through the *@poetartificial* account. *O Poeta Artificial* is built on top of PoeTryMe (Gonçalo Oliveira, 2012), a poetry generation platform, and originally used the latter for producing poetry from a set of frequent keywords in tweets that mentioned the target trend. *O Poeta Artificial* 2.0, hereafter shortened to *Poeta* 2.0, resulted from recent developments on the original version, aimed at increasing the interpretability of its results through a higher connection with the trend. The new features enable the reutilisation of fragments of human-produced tweets, possibly with a word replaced by its synonym, as well as the inclusion of fragments that highlight the trend, or fragments obtained from relations extracted from tweets about the trend, or even inferred from the latter. Produced poems may include some new fragments and others produced by the original procedure (hereafter, the classic way), based on the extracted keywords, while keeping a regular metre and favouring the presence of rhymes.

The remainder of this paper starts with a brief overview on poetry generation systems and creative Twitter bots, followed by a short introduction to PoeTryMe and how it is used by the Twitter bot. After this, the new features of *Poeta* 2.0 are described, with a strong focus on new kinds of fragments produced by this system. Before concluding, the results of *Poeta* 2.0 are illustrated with some poems produced, using different kinds of fragments.

2 Related Work

Automatic poetry generators are a specific kind of Natural Language Generation (NLG) systems where the produced text exhibits poetic features, such as a pre-defined metre and rhymes, together with some level of abstraction and figurative language.

Proceedings of the INLG 2017 Workshop on Computational Creativity and Natural Language Generation, pages 11–20,
Santiago de Compostela, September 2017.

Many poetry generators have been developed and described in the literature (see Gonçalo Oliveira (2017b)), especially in the domain of Computational Creativity. They are typically knowledge-intensive intelligent systems that deal with several levels of language, from lexical choice to semantics.

Several systems produce poetry based on given stimuli, which can be a set of semantic predicates (Manurung, 2003), one (Charnley et al., 2014) or more seed words (Gonçalo Oliveira, 2012), a prose description of a message (Gervás, 2001), or a longer piece of text, such as blog posts (Misztal and Indurkhya, 2014) or newspaper articles (Colton et al., 2012; Rashel and Manurung, 2014; Toivanen et al., 2014; Tobing and Manurung, 2015; Gonçalo Oliveira and Alves, 2016). Longer documents used as inspiration can be reflected in the poems through the use of keywords (Rashel and Manurung, 2014), associations (Toivanen et al., 2014), phrases (Charnley et al., 2014), similes (Colton et al., 2012), dependency (Tobing and Manurung, 2015) or semantic relations (Gonçalo Oliveira and Alves, 2016) extracted from them, and may also transmit the same sentiment (Colton et al., 2012) or emotions (Misztal and Indurkhya, 2014). Poems are typically built from templates, either handcrafted or extracted from human-produced poems, then filled with information from the inspiration document.

Twitter has become a popular platform for bots, mostly because of its nature – many users posting short messages (tweets), available on real time – and its friendly API, which exposes much information, easily used by computational systems. This is also true for creative bots. Some use Twitter merely as a showcase for exhibiting their results, possibly enabling some kind of user interaction, liking or retweeting. Those include, for instance, bots for producing riddles (Guerrero et al., 2015) or Internet Memes (Gonçalo Oliveira et al., 2016). Other bots also exploit information on Twitter for producing their contents. This happens, for instance, for *@poetartificial* (Gonçalo Oliveira, 2016), which produces poetry, in Portuguese, roughly inspired by current trends, and is the focus of the following sections. It is also the case of *@MetaphorMagnet* (Veale et al., 2015) and its "brother" bots, who produce novel metaphors, through the same generating mechanisms as a poetry generation system (Veale, 2013), more focused on content and not so much on form.

Despite the growing number of intelligent bots, Twitter has many other bots, some of which performing tasks that are typically in the domain of creativity, but through not so intelligent and knowledge-poor processes. Those include *@MetaphorMinute*, which generates random metaphors, or *@pentametron*, which retweets pairings of random rhyming tweets, both with ten metrical syllables.

Besides bots, other creative systems produce content inspired by information circulating on Twitter, including poetry. FloWr (Charnley et al., 2014) is a platform for implementing creative systems, which has been used for producing poetry by selecting phrases from human-produced tweets, based on sentiment and theme, and organising them according to a target metre and rhyme. TwitSonnet (Lamb et al., 2017) builds poems with tweets retrieved with a given keyword in a time interval, scored according to the poetic criteria of: reaction (presence of words that transmit a desired emotion), meaning (presence of given keywords and frequent tri-grams), and craft (metre and rhyme, plus words with strong imagery). Several poems by TwitSonnet were posted on Tumblr, another micro-blogging social network. Instead of templates, the previous systems reuse complete text fragments extracted from Twitter.

3 PoeTryMe and *O Poeta Artificial*

O Poeta Artificial (Gonçalo Oliveira, 2016) is a Twitter bot that tweets poems written in Portuguese and inspired by recent trends in the Portuguese Twitter community. It is built on top of PoeTryMe (Gonçalo Oliveira, 2012), a poetry generation platform with a modular architecture, so far adapted to produce poetry in different languages and from different stimuli.

PoeTryMe's architecture, explained in detail elsewhere (Gonçalo Oliveira et al., 2017), is based on two core modules – a Generation Strategy and the Lines Generator – and some complementary ones. To some extent, a parallelism can be made between this architecture and the traditional 'strategy' and 'tactical' components of a NLG system (Thompson, 1977). The Generation Strategy implements a plan

Proceedings of the INLG 2017 Workshop on Computational Creativity and Natural Language Generation, pages 11–20,
Santiago de Compostela, September 2017.

for producing poems according to user-given parameters. It may have different implementations and interact with the Syllable Utils for metre scansion and rhyme identification. The Lines Generator interacts with a semantic network and a context-free grammar for producing semantically-coherent fragments of text, to be used as lines of a poem. Each of those lines will generally use two words that, in the semantic network, are connected by some relation R. Those words fill a line template, provided by the grammar, which is generalised to suit all pairs of words related by R. For instance, the line template `you're the X of my Y` can be used for rendering partOf relations, such as:

- estuary partOf river
  → *you're the estuary of my river*
- periscope partOf submarine
  → *you're the periscope of my submarine*
- fiber partOf personality
  → *you're the fiber of my personality*

In most instantiations of PoeTryMe, a set of seed words is provided as input for setting the poem domain. This constrains the semantic network to relations that involve one of the seeds, with a probability of selecting also relations with indirectly related words (known as the 'surprise factor'). There is also a module for expanding the set of seeds with structurally-relevant words, possibly constrained by a target polarity (positive or negative). Though originally developed for Portuguese, poetry may also be generated in Spanish or English, depending on the underlying linguistic resources, namely the semantic network, the lexicons and the grammars (Gonçalo Oliveira et al., 2017).

O Poeta Artificial adds an initial layer for selecting the seed words to use. Before generation, it: (i) Selects one of the top trends in the Portuguese Twitter (the highest not used in the last three poems); (ii) Retrieves recent tweets (currently, up to 200), written in Portuguese and mentioning the target trend; (iii) Processes each tweet and extracts every content word used; (iv) Selects top frequent content words (currently, 4) to be used as seeds; (v) May expand the seeds, either according to the main sentiment of the tweets (based on the presence of emoticons) or, if there is a Wikipedia article about the trend, with content words from its abstract. PoeTryMe is then used for producing 25 poems from the seeds, following a generate-and-test strategy at the line level. The poem with the highest score for metre and presence of rhymes is tweeted.

In the original version of *O Poeta Artificial*, the result was always a block of four lines, generally with 10 syllables each, and with occasional rhymes. Due to their generation process, lines were syntactically-correct and semantically coherent, but the connection with the trend was often too shallow. For instance, as the trend is typically a hashtag or a named entity, it is not in the semantic network and thus never used in the poem. The following section describes recent developments towards a higher connection with the trend, thus contributing to an improved meaningfulness.

4 *Poeta Artificial* 2.0: beyond seed words

Poeta 2.0 aims at improving the meaningfulness of the original bot by increasing the connection of the produced poems with the target trend and with what people are saying about it.

A minor improvement occurs in the seed selection process. Instead of relying exclusively on the frequency of each content word in the tweets, *Poeta* 2.0 divides it by its frequency in a large Portuguese corpus (Santos and Bick, 2000). This aims to use more relevant words, and can be seen as an application of the *tf.idf* weighting scheme.

Yet, the main feature of *Poeta* 2.0 is that, besides seed words, it also provides a set of pre-generated text fragments to PoeTryMe, somehow connected to the target trend and that may be used as poem lines. For every line of the poem to fill, there is a probability of using one of the generated fragments instead of a line produced in the classic way, based on the semantic network and generation grammar. This probability is proportional to the number of fragments of this kind available for the target number of syllables. One of the previous fragments is also used if it has exactly the target number of syllables and rhymes with one of the previously used lines.

Another new feature is that, based on the produced fragments, *Poeta* 2.0 sets the target length of the poem lines, though having in mind the maximum of 140 characters a tweet can contain. More precisely, it counts the number of syllables of each text fragment produced and selects a number, between 5

Proceedings of the INLG 2017 Workshop on Computational Creativity and Natural Language Generation, pages 11–20,
Santiago de Compostela, September 2017.

and 10, for which there are more fragments available. Poems by *Poeta* 2.0 are still blocks of four lines, but each line will have the selected number of syllables or close.

The remainder of this section describes the different types of text fragments that *Poeta* 2.0 produces, namely fragments that highlight the trend, fragments of the processed tweets, paraphrases of the former, and fragments based on semantic relations. All are put together in a set of usable fragments. PoeTryMe will have no idea of how they were produced.

4.1 Fragments Highlighting the Trend

The first kind of fragments is based on a small set of templates with a placeholder for the target trend, each highlighting the latter by referring to it as a recent topic that many people are talking about. Some of those templates are shown in table 1, where T is the trend placeholder.

andam a escrever/falar sobre T (they are writing/talking about T)
hoje fala-se de T (today, people are talking about T)
sobre T vim escrever (about T I came to write)
interesse por T é global? (interest for T is global)
T é tendência social (T is a social trend)
T é um assunto recente (T is a recent topic)
fala de T muita gente! (many people chatting about T)
T, porque falam de ti? (T, why do they chat about you?)
T, T, e T (T, T, and T)

Table 1: Examples of trend-highlighting templates.

4.2 Fragments of Tweets

Similarly to other systems (Charnley et al., 2014; Lamb et al., 2017), *Poeta* 2.0 may reuse text from human-produced tweets. Recall that, in order to select the most relevant words for the target trend, 200 tweets written in Portuguese and mentioning this trend are used as an inspiration set. Among the processing steps, those tweets are broken into smaller units, when possible, following simple rules, such as line breaks or punctuation signs. Each of the obtained units is added to the set of fragments

Original fragment:
Salvador com dúvidas em aceitar (Salvador with doubts whether to accept)
Synonyms:
dúvidas = {*indecisões, hesitações, incertezas*} (doubts = {indecisions, hesitations, uncertainties})) *aceitar* = {*aprovar, acatar, adoptar*} (accept = {aprove, obey, adopt})
Paraphrases:
Salvador com <u>indecisões</u> em aceitar *Salvador com <u>hesitações</u> em aceitar* *Salvador com <u>incertezas</u> em aceitar* *Salvador com dúvidas em <u>aprovar</u>* *Salvador com dúvidas em <u>acatar</u>* *Salvador com dúvidas em <u>adoptar</u>*

Table 2: Tweet and some generated paraphrases.

provided to PoeTryMe. The main difference between *Poeta* 2.0 and other poetry generators that use human-written tweets is that *Poeta* 2.0 mixes them with the other kinds of fragments it produces.

4.3 Paraphrases of Tweets

Besides human-written tweets, *Poeta* 2.0 produces variations of them. More precisely, it retrieves synonyms of the content words in the previous fragments from PoeTryMe's semantic network, and produces new fragments by replacing each content word with one of its synonyms. *Poeta* 2.0 may thus find alternative ways of expressing the same messages humans did, possibly also covering a wider range of metres. This has similarities with Tobing and Manurung (2015), though *Poeta* 2.0 does not perform word sense disambiguation because PoeTryMe's semantic network is not organised in word senses. Although some issues may result from ambiguity, we prefer to think that, though not completely intentional, using synonyms that only apply for other senses may create interesting domain shifts. Table 2 illustrates this procedure for a specific fragment.

In order to avoid poems where all lines paraphrase each other, a maximum of 5 paraphrases are generated for each content word in a fragment. If a word has more than 5 synonyms, 5 are randomly selected.

4.4 Semantic Relation-based Fragments

In order to keep the philosophy behind PoeTryMe, the natural way of increasing interpretability would be to extract semantic relations from the tweets mentioning the trend and adding them to the set of relations to use. To some extent, we kept this philoso-

Proceedings of the INLG 2017 Workshop on Computational Creativity and Natural Language Generation, pages 11–20,
Santiago de Compostela, September 2017. ©2017 Association for Computational Linguistics

phy, but we also wanted *Poeta* 2.0 to be independent from the core of PoeTryMe. This enables the extraction of relations of different types, more focused on Twitter text, on the trends, and possibly not so well-defined, which can be managed without changing PoeTryMe. The same happens for a new set of line templates based on the extracted relations, smaller but more controlled than the line templates covered by PoeTryMe's grammars, most of which acquired automatically from collections of poetry.

Another important reason for this decision is that, in Portuguese, determiners, adjectives and other words are declined according to gender and number. In PoeTryMe, this is handled by a morphology lexicon and different grammar productions are still required, depending on the gender and number of the related words. Yet, while the same lexicon could be used for acquiring the gender and number of nouns or adjectives extracted from Twitter, it would not cover all the trends, which are typically named entities, or hashtags. Therefore, the templates for the Twitter relations are, as much as possible, gender and number independent, and only consider these attributes when they can be obtained from PoeTryMe.

In order to produce text fragments based on semantic relations involving the trend, *Poeta* 2.0 relies primarily on a small set of line templates compatible with each of the covered semantic relations. Yet, it goes further and combines the extracted relations with the relations in PoeTryMe's semantic network for inferring new relations and increasing, once again, the set of available fragments. The following sections describe the three steps involved in the production of relation-based fragments: extraction, inference, and text generation.

4.4.1 Relation Extraction

Since Hearst (1992) proposed a set of lexical-syntactic patterns for the automatic acquisition of hyponym-hypernym pairs from text, much work has targeted the automatic extraction of semantic relations from text, sometimes with much more sophisticated approaches. Yet, when recall is not critical, one of the arguments is fixed (the trend), and we are focused on a closed set of relation types, relying on a small set of lexical-syntactical patterns is probably the fastest way for achieving this goal. Moreover, it avoids the need for large quantities of encoded knowledge and provides higher control on the results than for machine learning approaches.

Currently, four different relation types are extracted from the inspiration tweets. This is performed with the help of a small set of patterns, revealed in table 3 and with possible results illustrated in table 4. In both tables, T stands for the trend, and a rough translation of the patterns, from Portuguese to English, is provided.

The extracted relations – isA, hasProperty, has, can – are tied to the extraction patterns but are not as semantically well-defined as relations in a wordnet or ontology. Yet, as long as we are aware of this in the following steps, it is not a critical issue.

4.4.2 Relation Inference

Based on the extracted relations, implicit in the text, other relations are inferred, when combined with relations in PoeTryMe's semantic network. For Portuguese, the network currently used includes all the relations in at least two out of nine Portuguese lexical-semantic knowledge bases, including wordnets and dictionaries (Gonçalo Oliveira, 2017a). Therefore, it covers a rich set of relation types including not only synonymy, hypernymy and partOf, but also others, such as isSaidOfWhatDoes (in Portuguese, *dizSeDoQue*), isSaidAbout (*dizSeSobre*), hasQuality (*temQualidade*), hasState (*temEstado*), antonymyOf (*antonimoDe*), isPart/Member/MaterialOf (*parte/membro/materialDe*), and isPartOfWhatIs (*parteDeAlgoComPropriedade*), which are exploited by *Poeta* 2.0

A set of rules was handcrafted for inferring new relations from a combination of one relation extracted from the tweets and another in PoeTryMe's semantic network. Although more inference rules may be defined in the future, possibly exploiting additional relations, the current rules are in figure 1. Again, the inferred relations are not as well-defined as those in a wordnet. Some are of the same types as the relations originally extracted, but new types are introduced (e.g. isLike, isNot, withQuality, withState, mayCause), some of which may result in metaphors or less obvious connections, and are thus useful for poetry generation. Table 5 illustrates some of the previous rules with examples of relations extracted, known (i.e. in PoeTryMe's semantic network), and inferred.

Proceedings of the INLG 2017 Workshop on Computational Creativity and Natural Language Generation, pages 11–20,
Santiago de Compostela, September 2017.

<table>
<tr><th>Pattern</th><th>Relation</th></tr>
<tr><td>... <T> (é|parece) (o|a|um|uma) <N> ...
(T is a/the N)</td><td>T isA N</td></tr>
<tr><td>... <T> (é|parece) <ADV> <ADJ> ...
(T is/seems ADJ)</td><td>T hasProperty ADJ</td></tr>
<tr><td>... tão <ADJ> (como|quanto) (o|a|um|uma)? <T> ...
(as ADJ as a/the? T)</td><td>T hasProperty ADJ</td></tr>
<tr><td>... <T> está <ADJ> ...
(T is ADJ)</td><td>T hasProperty ADJ</td></tr>
<tr><td>... <T> tem <N> ...
(T has N)</td><td>T has N</td></tr>
<tr><td>... <T> (está)? a <V> ...
(T is V-ing)</td><td>T can V</td></tr>
<tr><td>... <V> como (o|a|um|uma)? <T> ...
(V like/as a/the? T)</td><td>T can V</td></tr>
</table>

Table 3: Patterns considered and extracted relations.

Text	Relation
Bruno Mars é o rei do pop. *(Bruno Mars is the king of pop.)*	*Bruno Mars* isA *rei* (*Bruno Mars* isA *king*)
O Centeno é mesmo brilhante... *(Centeno is really brilliant...)*	*Centeno* hasProperty *brilhante* (*Centeno* hasProperty *brilliant*)
Wagner Moura foi tão sincero quanto Lula. *(Wagner Moura was as sincere as Lula.)*	*Lula* hasProperty *sincero* (*Lula* hasProperty *sincere*)
O António Costa está feliz da vida! *(António Costa is happy of his life!)*	*António Costa* hasProperty *feliz* (*António Costa* hasProperty *happy*)
Lorde tem talento demais. *(Lorde has too much talent.)*	*Lorde* has *talento* (*Lorde* has *talent*)
Manuel Serrão a pensar exatamente o mesmo que eu. *(Manuel Serrão is thinking exactly the same as I.)*	*Manuel Serrão* can *pensar* (*Manuel Serrão* can *think*)
Cantar como a Adele é dificílimo! *(To sing like Adele is so hard!)*	*Adele* can *cantar* (*Adele* can *sing*)

Table 4: Examples of extracted relations.

Extracted	Known	Inferred
T isA *rei* (king)	*real* (royal) isSaidAbout *rei*	T hasProperty *real*
T hasProperty *brilhante* (brilliant)	*brilhante* isSaidAbout *luminosidade* (light) *brilhante* hasQuality *brilhantismo* (brilliance)	T isLike *luminosidade* T isLike *brilhantismo*
T hasProperty *sincero* (sincere)	*sincero* hasQuality *sinceridade* (sincerity) *sincero* antonymOf *hipócrita* (hipocrit)	T withQuality *sinceridade* T isNot *hipócrita*
T has *talento* (talent)	*capaz* (capable) saidAbout *talento* *talento* isPartOfWhatIs *talentoso* (talented)	T is *capaz* T is *talentoso*
T can *pensar* (think)	*pensante* (thinker) saidOfWhatDoes *pensar* *pensar* causes *pensamento* (thought)	T is *pensante* T mayCause *pensamento*

Table 5: Examples of inferred relations.

4.4.3 Semantic Relations as Text

Both extracted and inferred relations are used for producing text fragments by filling, with the relation arguments, a small set of handcrafted templates, compatible with each relation type. Table 6 illustrates this with examples of fragments produced for a set of relations. Some fragments use both relation arguments, while others only use the second argument, and not the trend, to avoid much repetition.

5 Examples

This section presents some poems produced by *Poeta* 2.0, their rough English translations, and a short discussion on the fragments used. Despite the new features introduced, sometimes, poems still have all of their lines generated in the classic way. This happens especially when no tweets are reused, possibly due to their long size, and when no relations are extracted. The following poem is of this kind:

Proceedings of the INLG 2017 Workshop on Computational Creativity and Natural Language Generation, pages 11–20,
Santiago de Compostela, September 2017. ©2017 Association for Computational Linguistics

Relation	Example fragments	
Bruno Mars isA *rei*	*ser rei como Bruno Mars*	(being a king like Bruno Mars)
	por ser rei	(for being a king)
Centeno hasProperty *brilhante*	*quero ser brilhante como Centeno*	(I want to be brilliant like Centeno)
	dizem que é brilhante	(people say he's brilliant)
Lorde has *talento*	*Lorde tem talento*	(Lorde has talent)
	tem mesmo talento!	(she really has talent!)
Adele can *cantar*	*a cantar como Adele*	(singing like Adele)
	dizem que sabe cantar!	(people say she knows how to sing!)
Centeno isLike *luminosidade*	*Centeno lembra a luminosidade*	(Centeno resembles brightness)
	com uma luminosidade tal	(with such a brightness)
Lula withQuality *sinceridade*	*a sinceridade do Lula*	(Lula's sincerity)
	a demonstrar sinceridade	(showing sincerity)
Lula isNot *hipócrita*	*Lula não será hipócrita*	(Lula is probably not a hipocrit)
	nada hipócrita	(not a hipocrit)
Manuel Serrão is *pensante*	*Manuel Serrão parece pensante*	(Manuel Serrão seems to be a thinker)
	também quero ser pensante	(I also want to be a thinker)
Manuel Serrão mayCause *pensamento*	*como o pensamento de Manuel Serrão?*	(like Manuel Serrão's thought?)
	a gerar pensamento	(generating a thought)

Table 6: Relations and examples of produced fragments.

- If (T isA X) ∧
  - X isSaidOfWhatDoes Y → T can Y
  - Y saidAbout X → T is Y
  - X hasQuality Y → T withQuality Y
  - X hasState Y → T withState Y
  - X antonymOf Y → T isNot Y
  - Y isPart/Member/MaterialOf X → T has Y
- If (T hasProperty X) ∧
  - X isSaidOfWhatDoes Y → T can Y
  - X isSaidAbout Y → T isLike Y
  - X hasQuality Y → T withQuality Y
  - X hasState Y → T withState Y
  - X antonymOf Y → T isNot Y
  - Y hasQuality X → T isLike Y
  - Y hasState X → T isLike Y
- If (T has X) ∧
  - Y isSaidAbout X → T is Y
  - Y hasQuality X → T is Y
  - Y hasState X → T is Y
  - X isPartOfWhatIs Y → T is Y
- If (T can X) ∧
  - Y isSaidOfWhatDoes X → T is Y
  - X causes Y → T mayCause Y

Figure 1: Rules for relation inference

delatar sempre causa delação	To denounce always causes denunciation
delação negra sem acusação	Black denunciation without accusation
acusação em meia delação	Accusation in half denunciation
sem achar cita, nem citação	Without quotation or citation

It was generated for the trend *Carlos Alexandre*, the name of a Portuguese judge in charge of several cases with great public impact. All lines rhyme and all have 10 syllables, except the last, which has only 9. The seeds collected from the tweets were *delação* (denunciation), *advogada* (lawyer), *telefónica* (of telephone), *cita* (citation). The first line was produced from the semantic relation '*delatar* causes *delação*', the second and third from '*acusação* synonymOf *delação*', and the fourth from '*citação* synonymOf *cita*'.

The following example was produced on the morning of 4th of June 2017, after the attacks at London Bridge, when there was a trending hashtag *#LondonBridge*:

fala de #LondonBridge muita gente!	Many people talking about #LondonBridge!
O universo é mesmo doente	The universe is really sick
Polícia procura suspeitosos	Police searching for suspects
Polícia procura duvidosos	Police searching for dubious

All the lines have 10 syllables, except the first, because the syllable division tool considered the # as a syllable. Every line ends in rhyme: the first pair of lines ends in *-ente* and the second in *-osos*. The first line highlights the trend and the remaining are paraphrases of the following fragments from human-written tweets:

O mundo é mesmo doente (The world is really sick)

Polícia procura suspeitos (Police looking for suspects)

The next example was produced for the trend *Rui Santos*, a Portuguese football commentator, two days after Benfica won the Portuguese Football

Proceedings of the INLG 2017 Workshop on Computational Creativity and Natural Language Generation, pages 11–20,
Santiago de Compostela, September 2017. ©2017 Association for Computational Linguistics

Cup (30th May 2017). It uses three lines based on relations extracted from the processed tweets:

Rui Santos consegue falar
também posso ser miliar?
também quero ser miliar
seboso a par, par a par

Rui Santos can speak
can I be very small as well?
I also want to be very small
greasy at hand, parwise

All of its lines have 8 syllables and all have the same termination. The first line was produced from the relation '*Rui Santos* can *falar*' (talk), extracted from more than one tweet, including the following:

No lugar do Rui Vitória deixava o seboso do Rui Santos a falar sozinho com o seu troféu.
(If I were Rui Vitória, I would leave greasy Rui Santos talking alone with his trophy)

Another relation is '*Rui Santos* has *dimensão*' (dimension), extracted from:

Rui Santos tem dimensão para o Sporting. É pequenino.
(Rui Santos has dimension for Sporting. He is little.)

The second and third lines of the poem were produced from the relation '*Rui Santos* is *miliar*' (very small), inferred from the previous, due to the relation '*dimensão* isPartOfWhatIs *miliar*'.

The final example was produced for the trend *Ronaldo*, one day after the football player Cristiano Ronaldo won the fourth European Champions League of his career (5th June 2017). It mixes different kinds of fragments:

Ronaldo é muito falado
arte e dança amor calado
num estado de felicidade
Ronaldo mostra simplicidade

Ronaldo is widely spoken
art and dance silent love
in a state of happiness
Ronaldo shows simplicity

All lines have 9 syllables, with two rhymes: the first pair ends in *-ado* and the second in *-ade*. The first line highlights the trend. Due to a video of Ronaldo dancing, one of the seeds extracted was *dança* (dance), which originated the second line, based on the relation '*arte* hypernymOf *dança*'. The remaining lines result from two relations: '*Ronaldo* withQuality *simplicidade*' (inferred from '*Ronaldo* hasProperty *feliz*' and '*feliz* hasState *felicidade*'), and '*Ronaldo* withQuality *simples*' (inferred from '*Ronaldo* hasProperty *simples*' and '*simples* hasQuality *simplicidade*').

6 Concluding Remarks

In order to increase the connection between poems by a Twitter bot and a recent trend, more meaningful text fragments are now produced and, when possible, used in the poems. This paper described the production of those fragments.

The first impression of the poems now generated is positive, which is also shown by the examples included in this paper. Some poems are still produced in the classic way, where the only connection between lines and trend is the presence of associated words in semantically-coherent sentences. Yet, several have now lines that highlight the trend, lines that are built from relations involving the trend, or lines that reuse text by other users about the trend, thus making them more meaningful. Each kind of fragments may be further augmented, for instance, by exploiting additional patterns and semantic relations in the tweets, but the manual labour involved is a practical issue, as it may become quite complex to manage all the patterns and inference rules.

Another limitation is that the semantic relation-based fragments have to be gender and number independent. This may be minimised in the future, if the determiners frequently used before the trends are considered for identifying the previous properties. Yet, as there are other kinds of fragments, other relations, and poems only have four lines, this is currently not critical.

Most limitations of PoeTryMe (Gonçalo Oliveira et al., 2017) are also present. For instance, despite targeting the same semantic domain, lines are generated independently of each other, not always resulting in the most logical sequence. This could be minimised if a reordering procedure was applied, similar to the one by Lamb et al. (2017), where abstraction and imagery are considered.

The extraction of long-term information on the trend may also be improved. Currently, if the trend has a Wikipedia article, associations are extracted from its abstract. In the future, relations may be extracted directly from DBPedia.

A final issue, not yet discussed, is that the system may reuse fragments that contain typos, thus decreasing the quality of the poems. Of course, every word could be spellchecked and words with typos could be corrected, possibly to a different word than it should be, or their fragments could be discarded, possibly with many false positives.

As it happened for the original bot, every two hours, *Poeta* 2.0 tweets through the account *@poetartificial*, which has about 260 followers.

Proceedings of the INLG 2017 Workshop on Computational Creativity and Natural Language Generation, pages 11–20,
Santiago de Compostela, September 2017. ©2017 Association for Computational Linguistics

References

John Charnley, Simon Colton, and Maria Teresa Llano. 2014. The FloWr framework: Automated flowchart construction, optimisation and alteration for creative systems. In *5th International Conference on Computational Creativity, ICCC 2014*, Ljubljana, Slovenia.

Simon Colton, Jacob Goodwin, and Tony Veale. 2012. Full FACE poetry generation. In *Proceedings of 3rd International Conference on Computational Creativity, Dublin, Ireland*, ICCC 2012, pages 95–102, Dublin, Ireland.

Pablo Gervás. 2001. An expert system for the composition of formal Spanish poetry. *Journal of Knowledge-Based Systems*, 14:200–1.

Hugo Gonçalo Oliveira, Tiago Mendes, and Ana Boavida. 2017. Towards finer-grained interaction with a Poetry Generator. In *Proceedings of ProSocrates 2017: Symposium on Problem-solving, Creativity and Spatial Reasoning in Cognitive Systems*, Delmenhorst, Germany, July. CEUR-WS.org.

Hugo Gonçalo Oliveira. 2012. PoeTryMe: a versatile platform for poetry generation. In *Proceedings of ECAI 2012 Workshop on Computational Creativity, Concept Invention, and General Intelligence, Montpellier, France*, C3GI 2012, Montpellier, France, August.

Hugo Gonçalo Oliveira and Ana Oliveira Alves. 2016. Poetry from concept maps – yet another adaptation of PoeTryMe's flexible architecture. In *Proceedings of 7th International Conference on Computational Creativity*, ICCC 2016, Paris, France.

Hugo Gonçalo Oliveira, Diogo Costa, and Alexandre Pinto. 2016. One does not simply produce funny memes! – explorations on the automatic generation of internet humor. In *Proceedings of 7th International Conference on Computational Creativity*, ICCC 2016, Paris, France.

Hugo Gonçalo Oliveira, Raquel Hervás, Alberto Díaz, and Pablo Gervás. 2017. Multilanguage extension and evaluation of a poetry generator. *Natural Language Engineering*, page (in press).

Hugo Gonçalo Oliveira. 2016. Automatic generation of poetry inspired by Twitter trends. In *Knowledge Discovery, Knowledge Engineering and Knowledge Management (Post-conference Proceedings of IC3K — Revised Selected Papers)*, volume 631 of *CCIS*, pages 13–27. Springer.

Hugo Gonçalo Oliveira. 2017a. Comparing and combining Portuguese lexical-semantic knowledge bases. In *Proceedings of the 6th Symposium on Languages, Applications and Technologies (SLATE 2017)*, OASICS, page (in press). Schloss Dagstuhl - Leibniz-Zentrum fuer Informatik.

Hugo Gonçalo Oliveira. 2017b. A survey on intelligent poetry generation: Languages, features, techniques, reutilisation and evaluation. In *Proceedings of 10th International Conference on Natural Language Generation*, INLG 2017, page (in press), Santiago de Compostela, Spain. ACL Press.

Ivan Guerrero, Ben Verhoeven, Francesco Barbieri, Pedro Martins, and Rafael Perez y Perez. 2015. TheRiddlerBot: A next step on the ladder towards creative Twitter bots. In *Proceedings of 6th International Conference on Computational Creativity*, ICCC 2015, pages 315–322, Park City, Utah. Brigham Young University.

Marti A. Hearst. 1992. Automatic acquisition of hyponyms from large text corpora. In *Procs. of 14th Conference on Computational Linguistics*, COLING'92, pages 539–545. ACL Press.

Carolyn Lamb, Daniel Brown, and Charles Clarke. 2017. Incorporating novelty, meaning, reaction and craft into computational poetry: a negative experimental result. In *Proceedings of 8th International Conference on Computational Creativity*, ICCC 2017, Atlanta, Georgia, USA.

Hisar Manurung. 2003. *An evolutionary algorithm approach to poetry generation*. Ph.D. thesis, University of Edinburgh.

Joanna Misztal and Bipin Indurkhya. 2014. Poetry generation system with an emotional personality. In *Proceedings of 5th International Conference on Computational Creativity, Ljubljana, Slovenia*, ICCC 2014, Ljubljana, Slovenia, June.

Fam Rashel and Ruli Manurung. 2014. Pemuisi: A constraint satisfaction-based generator of topical indonesian poetry. In *Proceedings of 5th International Conference on Computational Creativity*, ICCC 2014, Ljubljana, Slovenia, June.

Diana Santos and Eckhard Bick. 2000. Providing Internet access to Portuguese corpora: the AC/DC project. In *Proceedings of 2nd International Conference on Language Resources and Evaluation*, LREC 2000, pages 205–210.

Henry Thompson. 1977. Strategy and tactics: a model for language production. In *Papers from the Regional Meeting of the Chicago Linguistic Society*, volume 13, pages 651–668, Chicago, IL, USA. Chicago Linguistic Society.

Berty Chrismartin Lumban Tobing and Ruli Manurung. 2015. A chart generation system for topical metrical poetry. In *Proceedings of the 6th International Conference on Computational Creativity, Park City, Utah, USA*, ICCC 2015, Park City, Utah, USA, Jun.

Jukka M. Toivanen, Oskar Gross, and Hannu Toivonen. 2014. The officer is taller than you, who race yourself! Using document specific word associations in

Proceedings of the INLG 2017 Workshop on Computational Creativity and Natural Language Generation, pages 11–20,
Santiago de Compostela, September 2017. ©2017 Association for Computational Linguistics

poetry generation. In *Proceedings of 5th International Conference on Computational Creativity*, ICCC 2014, Ljubljana, Slovenia, June.

Tony Veale, Alessandro Valitutti, and Guofu Li. 2015. Twitter: The best of bot worlds for automated wit. In *Proceedings of 3rd International Conference on Distributed, Ambient, and Pervasive Interactions*, DAPI 2015, pages 689–699, Los Angeles, CA, USA, August.

Tony Veale. 2013. Less rhyme, more reason: Knowledge-based poetry generation with feeling, insight and wit. In *Proceedings of the 4th International Conference on Computational Creativity*, pages 152–159, Sydney, Australia.

Proceedings of the INLG 2017 Workshop on Computational Creativity and Natural Language Generation, pages 11–20,
Santiago de Compostela, September 2017.

Template-Free Construction of Poems with Thematic Cohesion and Enjambment

Pablo Gervás
Instituto de Tecnología del Conocimiento
Universidad Complutense de Madrid
Ciudad Universitaria, 28040 Madrid, Spain
pgervas@ucm.es

Abstract

Existing poetry generation systems usually focus on particular features of poetry (such as rhythm, rhyme, metaphor) and specific techniques to achieve them. They often resort to template-base solutions, in which it is not always clear how many of the alleged features of the outputs were already present in the template employed. The present paper considers two specific features – thematic consistency, and enjambment – and presents an ngram based construction method that achieves these features without the use of templates. The construction procedure is not intended to produce poetry of high quality, only to achieve the features considered specifically in its design. A set of metrics is defined to capture these features in quantitative terms, and the metrics are applied to system outputs and to samples of both human and computer generated poetry. The results of these tests are discussed in terms of the danger of to ignoring certain features when designing construction procedures but valuing them during evaluation even if they arise from hard-wiring in the resources or serendipitous emergence, and the fundamental need for poets to develop a personal voice – fundamental for human poets and inconsistent with the application of Turing tests.

1 Introduction

Computer poetry generation has existed for some years now. Yet existing work in this field has very rarely applied existing techniques from natural language generation such as content planning, referring expression generation, lexical choice or surface realization. With the sole exception of Manurung's pioneering work (Manurung, 2003), attempts at computational poetry generation in the past have resorted to more generic artificial intelligence techniques, such as case-based reasoning, evolutionary programming or statistical language modelling rather than traditional natural language generation methods. At a lower level of granularity, these attempts operate more in terms of string manipulation than linguistic representation, and most of the solutions can be seen as template based generation. This is partly due to the properties of poetry, which, in contrast with prose, allows for evocative use of language that need not build complete sentences, but rather can get away with simple phrases concatenated into verse. Whereas this sort of tolerance is acceptable in the early stages of exploration of the field – when a poetry generator that could string simple phrases into verse was better than nothing –, at some point researchers interested in computer poetry generation need to consider the possibility of advancing beyond this.

The present paper considers a subset of the desired features of poetry as a text – thematic consistency, and enjambment – that are a (maybe optional) characteristic of human generated poetry but are often overlooked by computer generated poetry. A set of metrics is defined to capture these features in quantitative terms, and these metrics are tested on samples of both human and computer generated poetry. The results of these tests are discussed in terms of whether the features are indeed optional or whether they can help to distinguish instances

Proceedings of the INLG 2017 Workshop on Computational Creativity and Natural Language Generation, pages 21–28,
Santiago de Compostela, September 2017.

of simpler poetry from more elaborate examples. A new poetry generation system is proposed that specifically addresses some of the new proposed features and produces poems that score reasonably well on the proposed metrics.

2 Previous Work

The goal of this paper involves consideration of a number of poetic concepts establishing the subset of poetry-specific features that are being considered in the present paper (section 2.1), and a subset of the existing poetry generators that consider some of these features (section 2.2).

2.1 Definitions of the Poetic Features Considered

The idea that a given stanza should observe a *thematic unity* has been a classic consideration in traditional disciplines (Korpel and de Moor, 1998). In Arabic poetry, the lack of unity among the verses of a poem is denounced as a severe defect (Moreh, 1988). The formulation employed to justify this as a defect is that "In such poems it is possible to transfer a verse of one poem to another poem of the same meter and rhyme, or to change the order of the verses in the same poem without affecting the meaning or the subject". Consideration of this as a defect may be too strict even for most human poets. But it clearly establishes a criterion that may allow distinction of different degrees of elaboration for computer generated poetry.

Enjambment is a term used in poetry to describe cases where the meaning runs over from one poetic line to the next, without terminal punctuation (Baldick, 2008). Lines without enjambment, in which the syntactic unit (phrase, clause, or sentence) corresponds in length to the line, are called *end-stopped*. Enjambment has been identified as a sign of maturity in Shakespeare's poetry, with his later works distinguished by more frequent use of enjambment (McDonald, 2006). Although the correspondence between metric unit and syntactic units can be considered a positive feature, it seems reasonable to explore the possibility of establishing quantitative measures to identify the use of enjambment as an elaborate feature that requires skill and that many poets have considered an extremely positive feature which helps tie different lines together.

2.2 How Existing Poetry Generators Address the Features under Consideration

Explicit consideration of content as well as form in poetry was a distinguising feature of (Toivanen et al., 2012), developed to generate poetry in Finnish. This approach relied on corpus-based solutions for its generation task, and used separate corpora for form and content. Form was determined by a *grammar corpus* that provided instances of existing poetry that were adapted to create new poems by replacing some of their words with desired content. Content was determined by a *background corpus* from which a word association network for a user provided topic is mined based on word co-occurrences. The network is then used to provide candidate replacements for the words in the template selected from the grammar corpus, which leads to a certain thematic consistency. Because the templates are defined in terms of complete stanzas, the resulting poems do show instances of enjambment (as present in the grammar corpus). The reported version of the system does not consider rhythm or rhyme but mention is made of future work that would do so.

A different approach with potential impact on thematic consistency is the use of mood and sentiment in (Colton et al., 2012), which generated poetry in English. Here, a mood for the day is chosen at the start, then an article from the Guardian newspaper is chosen from which to mine keyphrase that will be combined with a template-based solution for complete stanzas over which rhythm and rhyme controls are imposed. The mood and the newspaper article provide thematic consistency, the template provides syntactic structure that sometimes involves enjambment.

PoeTryMe (Gonçalo Oliveira, 2012) generates poems in Portuguese inspired by a set of seed words by identifying semantic relations that the seed words might be involved in and building verses with spans of text that feature the two words involved in the semantic relation. Because all the verses in a poem are built from the same set of seed words, the resulting poems show a certain thematic consistency. It enforces conformance to a chosen metric. Its construction process is line-based, so it does not in principle allow for one line to syntactically connect to

Proceedings of the INLG 2017 Workshop on Computational Creativity and Natural Language Generation, pages 21–28,
Santiago de Compostela, September 2017. ©2017 Association for Computational Linguistics

the following one.

The work of (Veale, 2013) argues that prior poetry generators focus too much on rhyme and too little on having coherent content. To address this problem it uses a rich knowledge base of semantic relations between words mined from the Web. The resulting system produces poems in English that show thematic consistency and apparently insightful use of rhetorical figures such as similes, analogies and metaphor. Due to its specific choice of focus, this approach does not enforce conformance with metrical form either in terms of rhythm or rhyme, and it does not address enjambment.

A recent version of the WASP system (Gervás, 2016) addressed the interplay between theme and metric form in generated poems in Spanish over the conceptual space defined by an ngram language model extracted from a corpus of both poetry and prose texts. Generic guidelines were established to recognise regularity in rhythm and rhyme as valuable, but the system was allowed to explore the construction of stanzas of novel form as determined by the language model. Theme was very broadly stated and established by the choice of texts included in the corpus. The construction procedure is line-based with no mechanisms provided for identifying links between lines, so any enjambment in the resulting poems would be serendipitous.

The importance of evaluating thematic consistency in poetry generation has recently been emphasised by (Gonçalo Oliveira et al., 2017), which present a multilingual system capable of generating in Portuguese, Spanish and English. This work based on the PoeTryMe system evaluates – among other features – the semantic similarity between the generated poems and the seeds used to inspire them using PointWise Mutual Information (Church and Hanks, 1990). It also discusses the difficulties associated with applying metrics on poetic features across outputs in different languages, arising from the need of language-specific resources – lexicons, corpora, semantic knowledge bases ...– to inform any automated evaluation processes.

There has recently been a significant effort to address the task of poetry generation using solutions based on neural networks. Some of these initiatives consider explicitly the issue of thematic consistency.

The work of (Zhang and Lapata, 2014) presents a generator of Chinese classical poetry based on Recurrent Neural Networks. This system operates incrementally generating one line at a time, but at each point considers all previously generated lines as a context.

A different system (Yan, 2016) also uses RNN in an Encoder-Decoder with an iterative polishing schema to generate Chinese quatrains. This refines the poem in several passes by regarding the RNN's hidden state of the last line as the gist of the overall semantic representation of the poem.

In a more elaborate approach (Wang et al., 2016) address the problem in two stages, with an initial stage generating a plan for the poem – also in Chinese –, in which a particular subtopic specified as a chosen keyword is assigned to each line in the poem. The system then generates each line of the poem sequentially using a RNN Encoder-Decoder.

3 Poem Construction Aimed at Thematic Cohesion and Enjambment

From an engineering point of view, the existing work on automated poetry generation tends to select one particular feature of the desired inspiring set of poems and focus on developing a system capable of achieving results that satisfy that particular feature. This is usually done implicitly – with no explicit declaration of a decision to specialise on particular features. This approach allows the reader to imagine that the complete problem of poetry generation has been addressed – which may increase the perceived merit of the solution – but usually leads to disappointment and failed expectations when the outputs are considered. In this paper, the process being proposed focuses on the construction of rhyming poems with a certain degree of thematic cohesion and an ability to join up consecutive verses into syntactically acceptable phrases, which results in enjambment. This does not mean that any other features of poetry are ignored, but it does mean that any that appear in the results do so strictly by serendipity. It also means that the lack of any such additional features in the final results cannot be interpreted as a shortcoming of the system, because it is not designed to achieve those. If and when the engineering challenge of achieving the selected features is solved, the integration with techniques for achiev-

Proceedings of the INLG 2017 Workshop on Computational Creativity and Natural Language Generation, pages 21–28,
Santiago de Compostela, September 2017. ©2017 Association for Computational Linguistics

ing other features may be addressed. This is standard procedure in engineering and yet often ignored in the context of automated poetry generation. For the sake of methodological clarity, our contribution starts by defining a set of metrics intended to capture the features that we want our system to exhibit. A method for achieving results with those features is described, followed by a discussion of how well the proposed method fares under the metrics and in comparison with previous work.

3.1 Metrics for the Selected Features

The features that we intend to address are thematic cohesion and enjambment, as defined in section 2.1. The poetry under consideration should also address conformance to a given poetical tradition – which usually includes both rhythm and rhyme according to a classic stanza –, but this is not a feature under study in this paper. Conformance to poetical tradition has already been the goal of several research efforts, and it is not the main focus of this paper. Past efforts in the field have shown that such conformance is achievable algorithmically (see systems reviewed in section 2.2).

The features that we are considering could be measured automatically in different ways. However, the procedures for automating them would very likely be language dependent, as they usually need to rely heavily on linguistic resources. Even procedures based on corpora rather than explicitly declared knowledge are associated with specific corpora in the given language, which makes comparison across languages subjective even if an objective method has been followed (Gonçalo Oliveira et al., 2017). We will consider here metrics that rely on a human judge establishing the extent to which a given poem satisfies a given definition. This is less objective than any automated measure might have been, but it allows a measure of comparison across languages.

Thematic cohesion is a reasonably vague concept that everybody understands intuitively but which is difficult to pin down. For the purposes of this paper we will consider thematic cohesion in terms of co-occurrence within the poem of a number of words which can be considered to be semantically related in some way. To ensure that this broad sense of "related to theme" is captured, we have decided here to rely on a subjective definition of the relation as captured by the intuitions of a human evaluator. The metric is defined as:

$$TC = 10 * RN/TN$$

where TC is *thematic consistency* RN is the number of related nouns and TN is the total number of nouns.

Enjambment is a feature associated directly to the border between one verse and the next. A *line transition* is defined as the border between one line in the poem and the next. A line transition is considered *open* if the line after the transition can be considered a valid syntactic continuation of the line before the transition. These definitions allow the computation of the following metric:

$$EP = 10 * OLT/TLT$$

where EP is *enjambment percentage*, OLT is the number of open line transitions in the poem and $TLTV$ is the total number of line transitions.

3.2 A Generation Procedure Addressing the Features

In order to explore the level of difficulty involved in achieving poems that satisfy the proposed features, we have implemented a poetry generation module that targets these features specifically during construction. The SPAR (Small Poem Automatic Rhymer) system is based on observation of how human poets carry out their task. Namely with a strong base in the set of texts read by the poet before sitting down to write.

3.2.1 The Reference Corpus

SPAR generates based on a corpus of adventure novels that includes (Spanish versions of) *Tarzan of the Apes* by Edgar R. Burroughs, *Sandokan* by Emilio Salgari, *The Jungle Book* and *The Second Jungle Book* by Rudyard Kipling, *Peter Pan* by J.M. Barrie, *Alice in Wonderland* and *Through the Looking Glass* by Lewis Carrol, *The Prince and the Pauper* by Mark Twain, *The Hound of the Baskervilles* and *Study in Scarlet* by Conan Doyle. The choice of texts for the corpus was affected by two main reasons, one historical and one strategical. The historical reason is that the corpus had been compiled

Proceedings of the INLG 2017 Workshop on Computational Creativity and Natural Language Generation, pages 21–28,
Santiago de Compostela, September 2017. ©2017 Association for Computational Linguistics

previously to inform a poetry generation exercise in which primary school students were invited to interact with a poetry generator. For this purpose a set of texts considered classical readings for Spanish children had been chosen. The strategical reason is that it was decided that this set of prior readings should not include any poetry, so that the system allow testing of the ability of the system to generate verse inspired by a set of prose texts, and to avoid the risk that any poetic quality appearing in the resulting poems be directly attributed to a loan from poems appearing in the reference texts used as seed.

3.2.2 The Poetry Generation Process

SPAR carries out the poetry generation task in five separate stages. First, it builds from the reference corpus a series of models of which words in the available vocabulary appear next to others in the reference texts, and which words rhyme with one another. These models are used to inform later stages. Second, starting from a word provided by the user – which is intended to set the theme for the resulting poem – the system build a set of words related to the seed word. Relation in this context is defined in terms of simple cosine distance in a vector model representation of the reference texts (Salton et al., 1975). This set of words represent the concepts that the system considers might be mentioned in a poem that had the given word as a title. Third, it searches for connections between these words and potential rhyming words. A connection is understood to exist between words if they co-occur within the same window of N words in at least one of the sentence in the set of reference texts. Fourth, by exploring the search space determined by these connections the system builds phrases that might be included in a poem. These phrases are defined as spans of text that either connect target words to one another or a rhyming word to a target word. Each span is built by exploiting an n-gram language model of the reference texts to search for valid sequences of words that connect the desired words. Finally, for a given stanza, it searches for combinations of the resulting verses that satisfy the restrictions on rhyme and can be joined together with a minimum of cohesion. In this context, a minimum of cohesion is understood as having at least one ngram that overlaps the end of the first verse and the beginning of the second one.

3.3 The Resulting Poems

The SPAR system was used to generate a collection of 18 poems in Spanish. The poems were commissioned for the *Festival Poetas* poetry festival, celebrated in Matadero Madrid on 27-29 May 2017. The 18 poems were classical sonnets (14 verses of 11 syllables with rhyme schemes either ABBAABBACDCDCD or ABBAABBACDECDE). The design of the construction process ensures strict enforcement of this form. An example poem is presented in Table 1.

3.4 Applying the Metrics

In terms of the metrics defined in section 3.1, the SPAR system fares reasonably well. The current approach to publication of poetry generation research does not allow for collections of poems so built to be made available widely. This makes it difficult to carry out quantitative comparison between approaches, as only the data made available in each paper can be used. For comparison purposes, the proposed metrics have been applied to the sample poems published for some of the referenced poetry generators. Results for the SPAR collection in comparison with the poems published for some of the systems reviewed in Section 2.2 are presented in Table 2. For reference, results of applying the metrics to two different sets of Spanish poems are also included at the start of the table. These correspond to sets of four sonnets for classical 16th century poets (16C) and for 20th century poet Miguel Hernández (20C). The size of the sample has been selected to match that of available samples for computer generated poems.

As the various systems considered here were not originally design to address the issues on which they are currently being tested, it is important to qualify these numbers with some comments. The output of the system by (Colton et al., 2012) presents two types of poem, one based on a stanza-sized template and another based on loose chaining of independent lines. The results for enjambment in this case are not as meaningful as in other cases, because for one type the enjambment is inherent in the starting template and for the others it is non-existent. The system by (Toivanen et al., 2012) relies on stanza-sized templates for construction, so data on enjamb-

Proceedings of the INLG 2017 Workshop on Computational Creativity and Natural Language Generation, pages 21–28,
Santiago de Compostela, September 2017. ©2017 Association for Computational Linguistics

Por una mujer a la maldición.	For a woman to the curse.
De un hombre es un ser que les seguía.	Of a man is a being that followed them.
Miedo por la ley que no comprendía.	Fear for the law he did not understand.
Los celos hacia el mono y la expresión.	Jealousy toward the monkey and its expression.
Miedo por el hombre a una habitación	Fear for the man to a room
y el dios de la ley que no corría	and the god of the law that did not run
por un mono y el pueblo y que podía.	for a monkey and the people and who could.
Amo a esa mujer es su profesión.	I love that woman it is her job.
Quien amo y su mujer en mi carrera	Whom I love and his wife in my race
llega a ser que el hombre de no mostrar.	gets to be the man not to be shown.
Por un mono y la ley y el sonido	For a monkey and the law and the sound
que el dueño y el cachorro no tuviera.	that the owner and the cub would not have.
Sospecha que el cerebro y a juzgar.	She suspects that the brain and to judge.
Profundidades hasta que debido.	Depths until it is owed.

Table 1: Example of sonnet generated by the SPAR system for the seed word "Celos" (Jealousy).

	TC	EP
16C	7.2	8.8
20C	3.7	6.2
SPAR	5.2	4.8
(Colton et al., 2012)	2.9	1.3
(Toivanen et al., 2012)	3.0	2.0
(Veale, 2013)	8.1	0.0
(Gonçalo Oliveira et al., 2017)	3.7	0.0

Table 2: Results for samples of human (16C and 20C) and computer generated poems on the proposed metrics. In each case, average over the available set of poems in the sample is given.

ment refer directly to the chosen set of templates rather than the construction method. The system by (Veale, 2013) focuses explicitly on thematic consistency, and achieves very high scores on that, but has no concern about enjambment. The results on thematic consistency for (Gonçalo Oliveira et al., 2017) are heavily penalised by the fact that the metric only considers nouns, and should not be considered significant, as the poems do show additional indications of consistency in terms of verbs and adjectives.

4 Discussion

The application of the metrics to computer and human generated poems gives rise to some insights.

Thematic consistency is very difficult to evaluate. Simple perusal of the various poems gives a human reader a very solid intuition of whether a particular theme is being pursued, but this intuition is extremely difficult to quantify. Approaches that rely on automated means for extracting word associations from statistical analysis of corpora – such as (Toivanen et al., 2012) or the SPAR system itself– sometimes come up with word associations for which the rationale is very difficult to follow. This makes them score less well under human evaluation for consistency than they should, as they generally have followed strict construction procedures to achieve significant presence in their output of the desired words. System based on knowledge bases capturing semantic relations between words – such as (Colton et al., 2012), (Veale, 2013) and (Gonçalo Oliveira et al., 2017) – fare irregularly, with (Veale, 2013) – which focus specifically on thematic cohesion – achieving the highest score.

The proposed metrics relies exclusively on nouns, and should be extended to consider other types of words.

In comparison with the results provided for human generated poems, it might seem that modern poetry departs from the degree of thematic consistency shown by earlier poems. The problem that has been observed during application of the metrics is that the use of figurative language can significantly cloud the issue of consistency. Where the poet is working on one or more metaphors to illustrate his theme, a literal understanding of "is related to" will undermine his score even where a human reader will find obvious connections. In this sense, the set of poems used to represent 20th century poetry make heavier use of metaphorical associations. Further

Proceedings of the INLG 2017 Workshop on Computational Creativity and Natural Language Generation, pages 21–28,
Santiago de Compostela, September 2017. ©2017 Association for Computational Linguistics

work should address the role of metaphor in the application of metrics of this type.

The size of the samples is also problematic, both with respect to this particular measure and in general. For this type of quantitative metrics, application to a much larger sample would be desirable. This suggests that some means should be found in the field to associate with particular publications data sets of the resulting poems, so that this kind of empirical testing might be applied.

Concerning enjambment, the results on the metrics illustrate that the feature has been generally ignored by poetry generation systems in the past. It is also clear that the comparison between human and computer generated poems shows a significant gap with respect to this feature. Researchers working on poetry generation would do well to address this aspect specifically in future work.

Finally, the metrics as applied to the different systems considered here show that the use of templates, in spite of working considerably well regarding the quality of the outputs, is actually obscuring the fact that many significant issues underlying the task of poetry generation are being side-stepped. Enjambment as considered here is a case in point, but there may be multiple others in similar circumstances. In view of this, we advocate for a progressive transition from template-based solutions to more elaborate techniques for generating text. This may involve discovery of new methods of text generation, but it may also be achieved by more informed consideration of existing natural language generation techniques in the cause of poetry generation.

With respect to the SPAR system itself, a number of issues require comments.

Because the search spaces involved are so large, each of the stages described in section 3.2.2 can take between one and three hours of computing time. With smaller search spaces, the system might finish in shorter times, but the probabilities of finding valid combinations decrease in proportion. The density of correct verses that can be generated from a given (non-poetry) corpus is very low. This is what makes poetry generation so difficult. For these reasons, this particular approach to the automatic generation of poetry is not yet in a position to be used interactively.

The nature of the corpus – a set of adventure novels popular among young adults – has a strong influence in the results that can easily be perceived by anyone reading the poems. In contrast with poetry originating from other sources, the poems include frequent references to bears and wolves – Baloo and the Seeonee pack from the Jungle Book –, monkeys and lions – from Tarzan of the Apes –, a small bottle – as used by Alice – or to children's bedtime – the Darling children in Peter Pan. This peculiarity of the generated poems may make it less likely for readers to find connections between the poems and their own personal feelings, but it helps create an illusion of a joint general background and, in some sense, a particular voice for the automated poet.

Human poets dedicate a significant amount of energy to find a personal *voice*. This implies being able to produce poems that are significantly different from any others that had been produced before, and which can be attributed to that poet by someone familiar with their prior work. For a human poet, to have a part of their work declared indistinguishable from that of their peers, or – even worse – indistinguishable from the classics would be a radical sign of failure. This is an important issue for computer generated poetry, related to the expectation of originality traditionally associated with creativity. This is an important argument against the recent trend in the consideration of potentially creative outputs generated by computers to apply Turing test style evaluations, where success is associated with machine results being indistinguishable from human efforts. In the field of poetry, results indistinguishable from prior efforts are a sign of failure, not success.

The poems generated by the SPAR system cannot be confused with poems generated by a human. There is a clear tendency in them towards the surreal, an occasional warping of the rules of grammar to achieve metric correction, and a fixation with wild animals that arises from its background readings. That is in a way, the voice of the system. Maybe a relatively inmature voice at this stage, but clearly personal, different from what came before and recognisable once a number of poems have been read. To devote efforts to eliminate the small quirks that constitute at this stage the voice of the system would be detrimental to its perception as a poet with no significant advancement in terms of having modelled significant human abilities.

Proceedings of the INLG 2017 Workshop on Computational Creativity and Natural Language Generation, pages 21–28,
Santiago de Compostela, September 2017.

Possible improvements would be getting the system to become aware of more features of poetic texts to take into account – such as metaphor or aliteration – and to start operating with more elaborate definitions of purpose or intended message.

5 Conclusions

The use of templates in poetry generation leads to output poems of considerable quality, but clouds the actual capability of the systems in question to emulate fundamental abilities of human poets. Work in this field should progress away from the use of templates and make better use of existing natural language generation techniques.

Thematic consistency is very difficult to identify even for human judges, and it is therefore extremely difficult to automate. Any attempt to do so would need to find a solution for figurative use of language and the role of metaphorical connections in poetry.

Enjambment is a relevant and popular feature of human poetry that has not been addressed by poetry generation systems in the past. Metrics on enjambment can currently act as discriminators for human vs. computer generated poetry.

The use of Turing test evaluations for poetry generation is inconsistent with the basic tennets that define success and failure for human poets. Further effort should be made to evaluate computer generated poetry in ways that allow the attribution of quality independently of the ability to distinguish it from human poetry.

Acknowledgments

This project has been partially supported by project IDiLyCo (MINECO/FEDER TIN2015-66655-R), funded by the Spanish Ministry of Economy and the European Regional Development Fund.

References

C. Baldick. 2008. *The Oxford Dictionary of Literary Terms*. Oxford Paperbacks. Oxford University Press.

K. W Church and P. Hanks. 1990. Word association norms, mutual information, and lexicography. *Computational Linguistics*, 16(1):22–29, mar.

S. Colton, J. Goodwin, and T. Veale. 2012. Full-FACE poetry generation. In *Proc. of 3rd International Conference on Computational Creativity*, ICCC 2012, pages 95–102.

P. Gervás. 2016. Constrained creation of poetic forms during theme-driven exploration of a domain defined by an n-gram model. *Connection Science*.

H. Gonçalo Oliveira, R. Hervás, A. Díaz, and P. Gervás. 2017. Multilingual extension and evaluation of a poetry generator. *Natural Language Engineering*, page 1–39.

H. Gonçalo Oliveira. 2012. PoeTryMe: a versatile platform for poetry generation. In *Proc. of the ECAI 2012 Workshop on Computational Creativity, Concept Invention, and General Intelligence*.

M.C.A. Korpel and J.C. de Moor. 1998. *The Structure of Classical Hebrew Poetry: Isaiah 40-55*. Oudtestamentische Studiën. Brill.

H. M. Manurung. 2003. *An evolutionary algorithm approach to poetry generation*. Ph.D. thesis, University of Edimburgh, Edimburgh, UK.

R. McDonald. 2006. *Shakespeare's Late Style*. Cambridge University Press.

S. Moreh. 1988. *Studies in Modern Arabic Prose and Poetry*. E.J. Brill.

G. Salton, A. Wong, and C. S. Yang. 1975. A vector space model for automatic indexing. *Commun. ACM*, 18(11):613–620, November.

J. M. Toivanen, H. Toivonen, A. Valitutti, and O. Gross. 2012. Corpus-based generation of content and form in poetry. In *Proc. of 3rd International Conference on Computational Creativity*, ICCC 2012, pages 175–179.

T. Veale. 2013. Less rhyme, more reason: Knowledge-based poetry generation with feeling, insight and wit. In *Proc. of 4th International Conference on Computational Creativity*, ICCC 2013, pages 152–159.

Zhe Wang, Wei He, Hua Wu, Haiyang Wu, Wei Li, Haifeng Wang, and Enhong Chen. 2016. Chinese poetry generation with planning based neural network. In *Proceedings of 26th International Conference on Computational Linguistics*, COLING 2016, pages 1051–1060. ACL.

Rui Yan. 2016. I, poet: Automatic poetry composition through recurrent neural networks with iterative polishing schema. In *Proc. of the 25th International Joint Conference on Artificial Intelligence*, IJCAI'16, pages 2238–2244. AAAI Press.

Xingxing Zhang and M. Lapata. 2014. Chinese poetry generation with recurrent neural networks. In *Proceedings of the 2014 Conference on Empirical Methods in Natural Language Processing*, EMNLP 2014, pages 670–680. ACL.

Proceedings of the INLG 2017 Workshop on Computational Creativity and Natural Language Generation, pages 21–28, Santiago de Compostela, September 2017.

Synthetic Literature.
Writing Science Fiction in a Co-Creative Process

Enrique Manjavacas [1, 3]
enrique.manjavacas@uantwerpen.be

Folgert Karsdorp [2]
folgert.karsdorp@meertens.knaw.nl

Ben Burtenshaw [1, 3]
benjamin.burtenshaw@uantwerpen.be

Mike Kestemont [1, 3]
mike.kestemont@uantwerpen.be

Computational Linguistics & Psycholinguistics Research Center [1]
The University of Antwerp, Lange Winkelstraat 40-42, Antwerp, Belgium

Meertens Instituut [2]
Oudezijds Achterburgwal 185, 1012 DK Amsterdam, The Netherlands

Antwerp Centre for Digital Humanities and Literary Criticism [3]
The University of Antwerp, Prinsstraat 13, Antwerp, Belgium

Abstract

This paper describes a co-creative text generation system applied within a science fiction setting to be used by an established novelist. The project was initiated as part of The Dutch Book Week, and the generated text will be published within a volume of science fiction stories. We explore the ramifications of applying Natural Language Generation within a co-creative process, and examine where the co-creative setting challenges both writer and machine. We employ a character-level language model to generate text based on a large corpus of Dutch novels that exposes a number of tunable parameters to the user. The system is used through a custom graphical user interface, that helps the writer to elicit, modify and incorporate suggestions by the text generation system. Besides a literary work, the output of the present project also includes user-generated meta-data that is expected to contribute to the quantitative evaluation of the text-generation system and the co-creative process involved.

1 Introduction

In this paper we present ongoing work towards developing a text editing application, through which an established author of Dutch-language literary fiction will use an AI-based text generation system with the goal of producing a valuable piece of literature. Our aim is to create a stimulating environment that fosters co-creation: ideally, the machine should output valuable suggestions, to which the author retains a significant stake within the creative process.

The present project is part of a large-scale initiative by the CPNB ('Stichting Collectieve Propaganda van het Nederlandse Boek', 'Collective Promotion for the Dutch Book'). In Fall 2017, CPNB will launch their annual media campaign, which this year focuses on robotics. To this end, CPNB will distribute a re-edition of the Dutch translation of Isaac Asimov's *I, Robot* that is planned to include an additional piece written as part of a human-machine collaboration.

This project report is structured as follows. We first introduce the CPNB in greater detail, with special emphasis on their annual media campaign. We go on to introduce this year's 'Robotics' theme, and the way it centers around Asimov's *I, Robot*. Then, we concisely survey the state of the art in text generation from the point of view of co-creation between human and machine. Next, we describe our current

Proceedings of the INLG 2017 Workshop on Computational Creativity and Natural Language Generation, pages 29–37,
Santiago de Compostela, September 2017.

text generation system, starting with the large body of Dutch-language fiction (4000+ novels) that is at the basis of our experiments, as well as its preprocessing. We describe our choice of architecture for Natural Language Generation (NLG)—a character-level Language Model (LM) based on Recurrent Neural Networks (RNN) with attractive properties for the present task — and discuss how author and genre-specific voices can be implemented through fine-tuning of pre-trained LMs. We present ample examples to illustrate the model's output for various settings. We also discuss possible ways to evaluate our system empirically—a common bottleneck of text generation systems—, through the monitoring of user's behavior and selectional preferences. Finally, we discuss the design of the interface of our application, emphasizing various ways in which the author will be able to interact with the software.

1.1 Trust for the Collective Promotion of the Dutch-language Book

The CPNB[1] is a trust and PR agency based in The Netherlands that aims to promote the visibility of books and the publishing sector in Dutch society at large. The agency is responsible for a number of high-visibility annual initiatives, such as the 'Boekenbal' ('Book ball') and Boekenweek ('Book week').

These initiatives often center around specific themes. For the 2017 campaign *Nederland leest* ('The Netherlands reads'), the CPNB chose 'robotics' as the overarching theme for their campaign. Thereby further exacerbating the debate as the societal opportunities and challenges that come with the increase of artificial intelligence in everyday life, as well as literature. The campaign, for instance, includes the distribution of promotional material for children (see Figure 1), as well as copies of *I, Robot* (1950)—the well-known science fiction novel by Isaac Asimov—in its Dutch translation *Ik, Robot* (1966) by Leo Zelders, which serves as the focal point of the 2017 campaign. The novel is composed of interrelated short stories, prepublished in the journal *Astounding Science Fiction* between 1940 and 1950. They revolve around the fictional character of robot-psychologist Dr. Susan Calvin. The novel is especially famous because of the 'Three Laws of Robotics' which feature as an intriguing ethical backdrop.

The CPNB wanted to encourage debate about the role of AI and robotics in literature through the addition of a 10th short story co-created by an established fiction writer and a machine. An award-winning Dutch author, Ronald Giphart, agreed to take part in this experiment.

Figure 1: Make-it-yourself cardboard robot. Promotional material distributed as part of the 2017 'Nederland leest!' campaign by the CPNB on robotics and books.

1.2 Co-creativity

Co-creativity is a collaborative process between multiple agents, where in this context, one agent is a computational system. Davis sees co-creativity as the 'blending' of improvisational forces (Davis, 2013). This goes against the pragmatic distributional of labor that we might see in creative support

[1] Stichting Collectieve Propaganda van het Nederlandse Boek: `https://www.cpnb.nl`.

Proceedings of the INLG 2017 Workshop on Computational Creativity and Natural Language Generation, pages 29–37,
Santiago de Compostela, September 2017.

systems, or how computers are treated in everyday life, and invites them into an indistinct and overlapping process of creativitiy. Where crucially, the result of the output is greater than 'the sum of its parts' (Davis, 2013).

Interestingly, as pointed out by existing literature (Lubart, 2005; Davis, 2013; Jordanous, 2017), the public are suspicious of systems that purport to be autonomous whilst in fact involve human participation. Whilst for Lubart the opposite is the case. Lubart reorientates the scientific perception of these systems into one aligned with Human Computer Interaction, where they are examples of successful facilitators of improvisation (Lubart, 2005). Lubart clarifies co-creativity into four distinct roles for a computational system; 'Computer as nanny', 'Computer as penpal', 'Computer as coach', 'Computer as colleague' (Lubart, 2005, p. 366). In this project we are most interested in achieving the last, though in practice, much of what our system does could be considered under the second. For a more thorough overview of co-creativity and its role within computational creativity research, see the proceeding of The International Conference on Computational Creativity 2012 (Maher, 2012), and for a broader of view of the term in relation to computing, look to the work of Edmonds and Candy (Edmonds et al., 2005; Candy and Edmonds, 2002).

Developing NLG systems within a co-creative environment allows researchers to utilize the human agent within the system's workflow, allowing for approaches that are potentially too experimental for a solely computational approach. Furthermore, co-creation adds a collaborative and challenging dimension to the process of writing, which in turn encourages the human writer. That said, though collaboration is commonplace in writing, it is not always welcome. The creative process of writing is associated with a fluidity that can easily be hindered or broken; Umberto Eco's renowned 'How to write a thesis' asserts that writers should nurture their process (Eco, 2015). In developing this system alongside novelist Ronald Giphart, we sought to apply our work within his established methodology in a way that enriches both parties.

From a technical point of view, there is a possibility to limit the collaborative NLG system to an assistive role, solely aiding the writer. However, a valid collaboration should provoke and challenge the writer. It should test them, push them, and ask them to reconsider their approach. To achieve this balance we chose to treat the writer as a competent handler of text, completely capable of dealing with generated language, and unlikely to be overwhelmed. This approach certainly would not work for all applications, but seems appropriate to a professional science fiction writer.

As Natural Language Generation develops into a useful instrument in the creation of fictional prose, inherent questions arise around how computational systems relate to human writers. Nowhere else are these questions more at home than in science fiction literature, where readers and writers are eager to explore the speculative limits of technology. This willingness allowed us to consider the practical implications and qualities of co-creative writing, and how they manifest within the interface itself (see Section 4).

2 Related Work

Natural Language Generation within a collaborative writing environment is an active area of research. The co-creative setting gives scope to apply experimental approaches within the dynamic context of a working process. Here we will outline two established approaches: the structural diagramatic approach, and the auto-completion approach. Ahn, Morbini and Gordon use causal graphs to map the narrative steps of a story which the writer can manipulate into the eventual story structure, the system will then use probabilistic modeling to generate language around that skeleton. This approach gives the system access to the abstract narrative core of a story's structure; arguably, in doing so the system imposes upon the writer a far more structured approach than they are likely familiar with. A collaborative system should be able to fit within a writers existing working process (Ahn et al., 2016). Roemelle and Gordon offer a more hands on approach to assistive writing. Their system acts as a 'Narrative Auto-Completion', where the writer is prompted with possible sentences (Roemmele and Gordon, 2015). Though straightforward, this approach is highly intuitive and unobtrusive; however, the system risks fulfilling the role of tool rather than

Proceedings of the INLG 2017 Workshop on Computational Creativity and Natural Language Generation, pages 29–37,
Santiago de Compostela, September 2017. ©2017 Association for Computational Linguistics

collaborator. As such, Creative Help is a retrieval-based system, as appose to the generative approach presented below.

Narrative generation has been a central topic of computational creativity for decades. One of the first examples is Tale-Spin, a system that generates Aesop's Fables guided by a user's keyword suggestions (Meehan, 1977). More recently and nearer to this project, McIntyre and Lapata developed a probabilistic narrative generator that uses user-input to retrieve related phrases (McIntyre and Lapata, 2009). The system here differentiates itself from those by working on the character level. Generated text reproduces the style and voice of its training material, but does not directly sample quotes verbatim from the training material.

3 Method

3.1 Collection and Preprocessing

The first step in constructing our NLG system was to compile a sufficiently large corpus of literary works. In the present study, we employ a large collection of Dutch novels in epub format (Williams, 2011), which contains a diverse set of novels in terms of genre, and is heterogeneous in style. In total, the collection consists of 4,392 novels, written by approximately 1,600 different authors. The average number of novels written by each author is 2.5. The large standard deviation of 6.5 is caused by the skewed distribution in which a few authors contribute relatively large oeuvres, such as detective writer Appie Baantjer. The novels were tokenized for words, sentences and paragraphs using the Tokenizer Ucto, which was configured for the Dutch language (Van Gompel et al., 2012). The total number of sentences, words and characters in the tokenized collection (including punctuation) amounts to approximately 24.6M, 425.5M, and 2.1G, respectively. On average, each novel consists of 3k sentences, 59k words, and 309,531k characters.

3.2 Character-level Language Models for NLG

The aim of this project is to contribute to literary writing in a co-creative environment, as opposed to solely narrative generation. Therefore, we approach NLG using character-based Language Models (LM) which typically reason at a local level, in the order of some few hundreds of characters. Because of this, the LM is only implicitly aware of the global narrative structure, but still powerful enough to capture sentence semantics in a unsupervised fashion.

An LM is a probabilistic model of linguistic sequences that estimate a probability distribution over a given vocabulary conditioned on the previous text (left-to-right model). More formally, at a given step t, an LM defines a conditional probability, expressing the likelihood that a certain vocabulary item (typically a word or character) will appear next:

$$LM(w_t) = P(w_t|w_1, w_2, ..., w_{t-2}, w_{t-1}) \quad (1)$$

Different LM implementations exist, which diverge in the manner in which they model the previous text. Given their probabilistic nature, LMs are straightforward to deploy for NLG. The generative process is defined by sampling a character from the output distribution at step t, which is then recursively fed back into the model, potentially preceded by the previous output of the model, to condition the next generation at step $t+1$. A few decoding approaches can be implemented based on different sampling strategies. For instance, a rather naive approach towards sampling is to select each character so as to maximize a generated sequence's overall probability. Nevertheless, for a large vocabulary size (e.g. in the case of a word-level model), the search soon becomes infeasible; therefore, approximate decoding methods, such as beam search, are used to find an ideal solution. When used for generation, the naive *argmax* decoding strategy has a tendency towards relatively repetitive sentences, that are too uninspiring to be of much use in a creative setting. For the present work, we therefore decode new characters via sampling from the multinomial distribution at each step.

It is interesting to note that the different decoding approaches stand in a trade-off relationship between diversity and correctness. For example, whereas *argmax* decoding will tend to generate sentences that are very similar, general and monotonous yet formally correct (e.g. more similar to the sentences observed in the training corpus), multinomial sampling will make the output diverge more from the original training data, and therefore produce a more varied output, with a tendency towards formally incorrect sentences. Focusing on our chosen

Proceedings of the INLG 2017 Workshop on Computational Creativity and Natural Language Generation, pages 29–37,
Santiago de Compostela, September 2017.

approach—multinomial sampling—, the described trade-off can be operationalized and used to our advantage by letting the author explore model parameters. This is implemented by exposing a parameter τ, commonly referred to as "temperature", that controls the skewness of the model's output distribution. Given the output distribution at a given step $p = (p_1, p_2, ..., p_V)$, a vocabulary size of V, and the temperature value τ, we can compute a transformation of p^τ of the original p through Equation 2

$$p_i^\tau = \frac{p_i^{\frac{1}{\tau}}}{\sum_j^V p_j^{\frac{1}{\tau}}} \tag{2}$$

p^τ will flatten the original distribution for higher values of τ— thereby ensuring more variability in the output. Conversely, for lower values of τ it will skew the distribution—thereby facilitating the outcome of the originally more probable symbol. For τ values approaching zero, we recover the simple argmax decoding procedure of picking the highest probability symbol at each step, whereas for high enough τ the LM degenerates into a random process in which at any given step all symbols are equally probable regardless of the history.

In terms of implementations there are two major approaches to statistical language modeling—ngram-based LMs and RNN-based LMs.

3.2.1 Ngram Language Models

Ngram-based LMs (NGLMs) go back to at least the early 1980s in the context of Statistical Machine Translation and Speech Recognition (Rosenfeld, 2000). An NGLM is a direct application of the Markov assumption to the task of estimating the next character probability distribution—e.g. it uses a fixed-length ngram prefix to estimate the next character probability distribution. An NGLM is basically a conditional probability table for Equation 1 , that is estimated on the basis of the count data for ngrams of a given length n. Typically, NGLMs suffer from a data sparsity problem, because with larger values of n possible conditioning prefixes will not be observed in the training data and the corresponding probability distribution cannot be estimated. To alleviate the sparsity problem, techniques such as smoothing and back-off models (Chen and Goodman, 1999) can be used to either reserve some probability mass to redistribute it across unobserved ngrams (smoothing), or resort back to a lower-order model to provide an approximation to the conditional distribution of an unobserved ngram (back-off models).

3.2.2 RNN-based Language Models

More recently, a new class of LMs based on Recurrent Neural Networks (Elman, 1990) have been introduced (Bengio et al., 2003; Mikolov, 2012) and have quickly increased in popularity due to their better theoretical properties (no Markov assumption), expressive capabilities (information flow through very long sequences) and performance gains. An RNNLM processes an input sequence one step t at a time, feeding the input symbol x_t through three affine transformations with their corresponding non-linearities. First, the one-hot encoded input vector is projected into an embedding space of dimensionality M through $w_t = W^m x_t$, where $W^m \in \mathbb{R}^{MxV}$ is a embedding matrix. Secondly, the resulting character embedding w_t is fed into an RNN layer that computes a hidden activation h_t as a combination of w_t with the hidden activation of the previous step h_{t-1}. This is shown formally in Equation 3

$$h_t = \sigma(W^{ih} w_i + W^{hh} h_{t-1} + b_h) \tag{3}$$

where $W^{ih} \in \mathbb{R}^{MxH}$ and $W^{hh} \in \mathbb{R}^{HxH}$ are respectively the input-to-hidden and hidden-to-hidden projection matrices, b_h is a bias vector and σ is the sigmoid non-linear function. Finally, the hidden activation h_t is projected into the vocabulary space of size V, followed by a *softmax* function that turns the output vector into a valid probability distribution. Formally, the probability of character j at step t is defined by

$$P_{t,j} = \frac{e^{o_{t,j}}}{\sum_k^V e^{o_{t,k}}} \tag{4}$$

where $o_{t,j}$ is the jth entry in the output vector $o_t = W^{ho} h_t$ and $W^{ho} \in \mathbb{R}^{VxH}$ is the hidden-to-output projection.

In practice, training an RNN is difficult due to the vanishing gradient problem (Hochreiter, 1998) that makes it hard to apply the back-propagation learning algorithm (Rumelhart et al., 1986) for parameter learning over very long sequences. Therefore,

Proceedings of the INLG 2017 Workshop on Computational Creativity and Natural Language Generation, pages 29–37, Santiago de Compostela, September 2017.

it is common to implement the recurrent layer using an enhanced RNN version to compute h_t—such as Long Short-term Memory (LSTM) (Hochreiter and Schmidhuber, 1997) or Gated-Recurrent Unit (GRU) (Cho et al., 2014)—, which add an explicit gated mechanism to the traditional RNN in order to control the preservation of information in the hidden state over very long sequences.

3.2.3 Model

For the present study, we implement several variations of the RNNLM, varying the type of the recurrent cell (LSTM, GRU) as well as the values of different parameters, such as the dimensionality of the character embedding matrix W^m (24, 46, ...) and, more importantly, the size of the hidden layer H (1024, 2048, ...). We train our models through back-propagation using Stochastic Gradient Descent (SGD), clipping the gradients before each batch update to a maximum norm value of 5 to avoid the exploding gradient problem (Pascanu et al., 2013) and truncating the gradient during back-propagation to a maximum of 200 recurrent steps to ensure sufficiently long dependencies in the sequence processing. Finally, dropout (Srivastava et al., 2014) is applied after each recurrent layer following (Zaremba et al., 2015) to prevent overfitting during full model training.

3.2.4 Overfitting

After training the full model, we experiment with further fine-tuning on different author and genre specific subsets to steer the NLG towards a particular style. To enforce this effect, we drive the training towards overfitting introducing an intended bias in the models predictions towards sequences that are more likely in that particular book subset. We achieve overfitting by zeroing the dropout rate and running numerous passes through the subset training data, with a sufficiently small learning rate. We have already observed interesting stylistic and genre properties in the fine-tuned model's output—see Section 4.2 for an illustration. That said, how the particular effect of this technique—differing degrees of overfitting—affects the quality of the generated output still has to be evaluated. The degree of overfitting can easily be quantified and monitored by plotting batched-average perplexity values achieved by the model for both the training data and the validation split as shown in Figure 2.

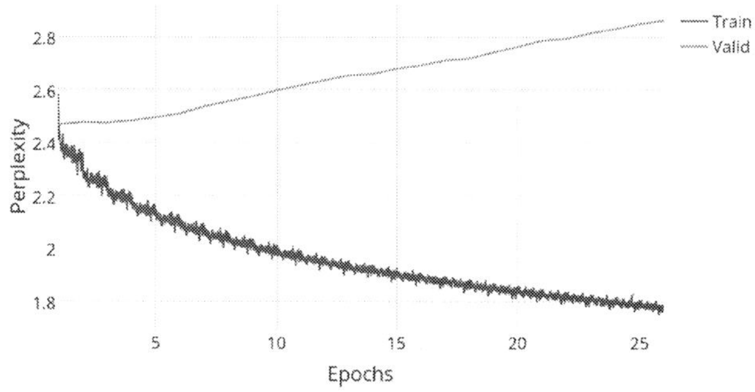

Figure 2: Example of overfitting learning curves during fine-tuning of a full model on a subset of novels by Isaac Asimov.

4 User Interface

Uncharacteristically for an NLP project, the visual interface of the system is paramount to its success. Though ultimately the system will be assessed on the language it produces, such language can only be generated if the writer is able to use the system. Therefore, we have focused on functionalities that give the user a clear representation of how text is generated, and allow them to understand how their own writing is affected by the process. This allows them to play a defined role within the process of writing, whilst also encouraging them to use generated text. The user is able to select which model to generate text from, so that they can use multiple voices and approaches within the same text (see Section 3.2.4). The user can define 'temperature' for any model using a slider bar (see Section 3.2). The generated text itself is shown as a list of suggestions, along with the model's own probability scores, below the main text area. This allows the writer to choose between a set of options, and get a broader idea of the models voice. With the help of user edit meta-data—computed by a string *diffing* algorithms—we can track user changes and present them with a visualization of each fragment's source and the degree of the modification.

Figure 3 is a visual representation of how text annotation functions. Text annotation reveals to the writer how generated text is affecting the final text. As the writer works into text, they could easily lose

Proceedings of the INLG 2017 Workshop on Computational Creativity and Natural Language Generation, pages 29–37,
Santiago de Compostela, September 2017. ©2017 Association for Computational Linguistics

Een paar dagen dacht ik na over deze ontmoeting en welke kant ik op moest om de zaak te verklaren. Ik dacht dat het misschien een vergissing was om een aanval te verwachten, maar dat was niet nodig. Ik was er zeker van dat hij niet alles verklaarde wat ik wist. Maar het was niet mijn bedoeling mijn pamflet te vernietigen. Het kon me niet schelen wat er gebeurde. Ik baalde dat hij me aan het lijntje hield en wilde hem niet meer zien. Ik had het gevoel dat ik niet voldoende wist om me te verdedigen en daarbij had ik geen idee wat hij van mij vond.
In korte tijd las ik alles wat er te lezen viel over humanoïde robots en de werking van de vier Machines die de Sferen onder controle hadden. Waarin zat mijn weerzin tegen hun alomtegenwoordigheid? En wat nu als ze oprecht het goede voor de mensheid wilden? De tegenstrijdigheid in de onzekerheid van hun manier van doen, die in mijn ogen een feit was, was niet alleen maar een stap voorwaarts. Ik had het gevoel dat ik me er niet van bewust was dat ik mijn eigen gang ging. Ik wilde het niet horen, maar ik wilde het. Ik wilde het. Ik wilde het niet.
En daarom updatete ik Moralis, mijn ethiekbot, want in de tien jaar dat ik hem voor het laatst had gevoed met inzichten en wijsheden was de wereld nogal veranderd.
'Wat moet ik doen?' vroeg ik hem, toen ik daarmee klaar was.

Figure 3: Visual feedback on the co-creation process used by Ronald Giphart. Highlighted fragments are synthetic in origin with the brightness indicating the amount of modification introduced by the user.

track of its source; therefore, the interface is enhanced with visual feedback which highlights based on edit distance between original generated text and its current status. Generated text is initially highlighted in green, as the writer edits that text its color fades into white. At the same time, whole words swapped by the writer are underlined in purple to differentiate lexical changes (see Figure 3).

4.1 Monitoring the Author

Our project intends to explore the co-creative process of science-fiction literature on a quantitative and objective basis. In line with (Roemmele and Gordon, 2015), we acknowledge that such a co-creative interface opens the up possibility for automatic evaluation of generative systems based on user edits of generated strings. Our interface is therefore designed to store all user edits along with the source of the string (human or machine generated). This will enable us to study individual user behavior in relation to the particular properties of the generative system, as well as the aptness of different model variants and their parameter settings (e.g. degree of overfit, temperature, voice) for co-creation, taking user edit behavior as a proxy for output quality.

4.2 Examples

As explained in the previous section, the evaluation of a NLG system in a co-creative setting involving both human and machine amounts to the generated material incorporated (either explicitly or implicitly) by the author in the final work. Suggestions about how to formally and informally evaluate this co-production process were given in the previous section. Here, we provide an exploratory demonstration of the model's generation system, where the goal is to highlight some typical behavior of the system under different parameters settings, author-based fine-tuning, and text seeds.

We begin with a survey of how different temperature values τ impact the generated text. In Table 1 we list a number of generated sentences for different temperatures given the famous opening sentence "Mijn vrouw is dood en al begraven" ('My wife is dead and already buried') from Marcellus Emants' *Een nagelaten bekentenis*. These examples have been generated on the basis of a model trained on the complete collection as described in Section 3.1. Several observations can be made from these examples. First, the examples showcase the model's ability to generate grammatical sentences. Interestingly, the sentences become syntactically more complex as the temperature increases (as explained in Section 3.2), and also exhibit less repetitive grammatical structures (cf. the repetition of possessive *van* constructions with $\tau = 0.1$). Second, a similar diversifying effect can be observed on the lexical level. Higher temperatures are more likely to generate less frequent and semantically more specific lexical material (cf. the decrease in reusing the same word twice, as well as the increase of names in the final two examples). Third, depending on the reader's willingness to search for semantic coherence, most generated sentences can be read as plausible continuations of the input seed. Finally, with increased temperature values the model composes sentences with higher semantic and cognitive complexity, juxtaposing and combining less common concepts and thoughts. Within certain limits, we expect such increased 'creativity' to encourage and provoke the human writer in the process of writing.

Proceedings of the INLG 2017 Workshop on Computational Creativity and Natural Language Generation, pages 29–37, Santiago de Compostela, September 2017. ©2017 Association for Computational Linguistics

seed / τ	Mijn vrouw is dood en al begraven.	My wife is dead and already buried.
0.1	*De volgende dag werd er een bericht van de politie gevonden. De verklaring van de politie was een van de belangrijkste verklaringen van de man die het verhaal van de politie had gehoord.*	*The next day, a police message was found. The police's statement was one of the most important statements of the man who heard the story by the police.*
0.3	*De dokter keek op zijn horloge. Ze was er zeker van dat hij die dag niet meer zou komen. Hij was niet gek. Hij was niet van plan om zijn dochter te vertellen dat hij haar een keer had gezien.*	*The doctor looked at his watch. She was sure he wouldn't come anymore that day. He wasn't crazy. He did not intend to tell his daughter he'd seen her once.*
0.5	*De tranen weerklonken over haar gezicht en voelde ze in haar keel. Ze was er niet. Ze was er zeker van dat ze alleen maar een affaire had gehad met de meisjes.*	*The tears resounded over her face and she felt them in her throat. She wasn't there. She was sure she had only had an affair with the girls.*
0.7	*Ze zegt dat het weer in San Sebastian naar Californië haar deel van de wereld is. Ze moet van de wereld naar de hemel hebben gelopen.*	*She says that the weather in San Sebastian to California is her part of the world. She must have walked from the world to heaven.*
0.9	*Lucas kon niet met zichzelf trouwen en toen hij achteloos met zijn gebaren zat te praten maakte hij deel uit van de lessen van de waarheid.*	*Lucas couldn't marry himself, and when he spoke painlessly with his gestures, he was part of the lessons of truth.*

Table 1: Example of our current NLG system with translation seeded by "Mijn vrouw is dood en al begraven" (My wife is dead and already buried) for different temperature τ values.

Having explored the impact of temperature on the full model's output, we now proceed with a brief illustration and informal evaluation of the generated output of two fine-tuned models. As explained in Section 3.2.4, we experiment with constructing fine-tuned models for specific styles, genres or authors by post-training on a subset of the collection and driving the training towards overfitting. In this section, we demonstrate the effect of overfitting two models post-trained on novels by Isaac Asimov and Ronald Giphart, who form the heart of the CPNB's robotics campaign. Using the same seed from Table 1, we observe a clear style shift when generating sentences using either the Asimov or Giphart model. For example, with a temperature setting of $\tau = 0.4$ the Asimov model produces utterances such as: "Mijn vrouw is dood en al begraven. *'Het is de grootste misdaad die ik ooit heb gezien.' 'Weet u dat zeker?' 'Ja.' 'En als dat zo is, wat is dan wel de waarheid?'* (My wife is dead and already buried. 'It is the biggest crime I've ever seen.' 'Are you sure?' 'Yes.' 'And if so, what is the truth?'). By contrast, a model overfitted on novels by Giphart generates output such as: "Mijn vrouw is dood en al begraven. *Ik heb het over een door mij gefotografeerde vrouw, een hoofd dat met haar borsten over mijn schouder ligt. Ik heb de film geschreven die ik mijn leven lang heb geleefd.*" ('My wife is dead and already buried. I'm talking about a woman I once photographed, a head with her breasts over my shoulder. I wrote the movie I've lived my life for a long time.') Both continuations are semantically plausible, yet written in completely different styles, and put focus on different concepts (e.g. 'crime' versus 'erotics'), both typical of their respective training material.

5 Conclusion

In this paper we have outlined an applied text generation system and graphical user interface, that together facilitate co-creative environment in which to write science fiction literature. We have highlighted an existing challenge within state of the art systems, to balance a challenging intervention into the writing process, with the risk of becoming a solely a writing tool. The character-level recurrent neural network for NLG that we have used is experimental within a solely computational approach, and therefore we have leveraged the specific advantages of working with a professional writer to maximize this system's ability to be applied. We have how to facilitate a writer to use a language model. We have outlined

Proceedings of the INLG 2017 Workshop on Computational Creativity and Natural Language Generation, pages 29–37,
Santiago de Compostela, September 2017. ©2017 Association for Computational Linguistics

evaluation procedures for the current NLG system, utilizing user-generated meta-data and quantifying the extent of retained synthetic text.

Acknowledgments

We would like to thank Ronald Giphart for his time and energy and Stichting Collectieve Propaganda van het Nederlandse Boek for initiating the collaboration.

References

Emily Ahn, Fabrizio Morbini, and Andrew S. Gordon. 2016. Improving Fluency in Narrative Text Generation With Grammatical Transformations and Probabilistic Parsing. In *The 9th International Natural Language Generation conference*, pages 70–74, Edinburgh, UK. ACL.

Yoshua Bengio, Réjean Ducharme, Pascal Vincent, and Christian Janvin. 2003. A Neural Probabilistic Language Model. *The Journal of Machine Learning Research*, 3:1137–1155.

Linda Candy and Ernest Edmonds. 2002. Modeling co-creativity in art and technology. In *Proceedings of the 4th conference on Creativity & cognition*, pages 134–141, Loughborough, UK. ACM.

Stanley F Chen and Joshua Goodman. 1999. An empirical study of smoothing techniques for language modeling. *Computer Speech and Language*, 13:359–394.

Kyunghyun Cho, Bart Van Merrienboer, Dzmitry Bahdanau, and Yoshua Bengio. 2014. On the Properties of Neural Machine Translation : Encoder – Decoder Approaches. *Ssst-2014*, pages 103–111.

Nicholas Davis. 2013. Human-computer co-creativity: Blending human and computational creativity. In *Ninth Artificial Intelligence and Interactive Digital Entertainment Conference*. AAAI Press.

Umberto Eco. 2015. *How to write a thesis*. MIT Press.

Ernest A. Edmonds, Alastair Weakley, Linda Candy, Mark Fell, Roger Knott, and Sandra Pauletto. 2005. The studio as laboratory: Combining creative practice and digital technology research. *International Journal of Human-Computer Studies*, 63(4-5):452–481, October.

Jeffrey L. Elman. 1990. Finding structure in time. *Cognitive Science*, 14(2):179–211.

Sepp Hochreiter and Jürgen Schmidhuber. 1997. Long Short-Term Memory. *Neural Computation*, 9(8):1735–1780.

Sepp Hochreiter. 1998. The Vanishing Gradient Problem During Learning Recurrent Neural Nets and Problem Solutions. *International Journal of Uncertainty, Fuzziness and Knowledge-Based Systems*, 06(02):107–116.

Anna Jordanous. 2017. Co-creativity and perceptions of computational agents in co-creativity. In *Proceedings of the Eighth International Conference on Computational Creativity*, Atlanta, US. ACC.

Todd Lubart. 2005. How can computers be partners in the creative process: Classification and commentary on the Special Issue. *International Journal of Human-Computer Studies*, 63(4-5):365–369, October.

Mary Lou Maher. 2012. Computational and Collective Creativity: Who's Being Creative? In *Proceedings of the 3rd International Conference on Computer Creativity*, pages 67–71, Dublin, Ireland. ACC.

Neil McIntyre and Mirella Lapata. 2009. Learning to tell tales: A data-driven approach to story generation. In *Proceedings of the Joint Conference of the 47th Annual Meeting of the ACL and the 4th International Joint Conference on Natural Language Processing of the AFNLP: Volume 1-Volume 1*, pages 217–225, Singapore. Association for Computational Linguistics.

James R. Meehan. 1977. TALE-SPIN: An interactive program that writes stories. In *Proceedings of the 5th International Joint Conference on Ar tificial Intelligence*, pages 91–98.

Tomas Mikolov. 2012. Statistical Language Models Based on Neural Networks.

Razvan Pascanu, Tomas Mikolov, and Yoshua Bengio. 2013. On the Difficulties of Training Recurrent Neural Networks. *Icml*, (2):1–9.

Melissa Roemmele and Andrew S. Gordon. 2015. Creative help: a story writing assistant. In *International Conference on Interactive Digital Storytelling*, pages 81–92. Springer.

Ronald Rosenfeld. 2000. Two decades of statistical language modeling: where do we go from here? *Proceedings of the IEEE*, 88(8):1270–1278.

David E. Rumelhart, Geoffrey E. Hinton, and Ronald J. Williams. 1986. Learning representations by back-propagating errors. *Nature*, 323(6088):533–536.

Nitish Srivastava, Geoffrey Hinton, Alex Krizhevsky, Ilya Sutskever, and Ruslan Salakhutdinov. 2014. Dropout: A Simple Way to Prevent Neural Networks from Overfitting. *Journal of Machine Learning Research*, 15:1929–1958.

Maarten Van Gompel, Ko Van Der Sloot, and Antal Van den Bosch. 2012. Ucto: Unicode Tokeniser Reference Guide. Technical report.

Greg Williams. 2011. EPUB: Primer, Preview, and Prognostications. *Collection Management*, 36(3):182–191.

Wojciech Zaremba, Ilya Sutskever, and Oriol Vinyals. 2015. Recurrent Neural Network Regularization. *ICLR*, pages 1–8.

Proceedings of the INLG 2017 Workshop on Computational Creativity and Natural Language Generation, pages 29–37, Santiago de Compostela, September 2017. ©2017 Association for Computational Linguistics

Constructing narrative using a generative model and continuous action policies

Emmanouil Theofanis Chourdakis and **Joshua D. Reiss***
Queen Mary University of London
Mile End Road, E1 4NS
London, UK
{e.t.chourdakis, joshua.reiss}@qmul.ac.uk

Abstract

This paper proposes a method for learning how to generate narrative by recombining sentences from a previous collection. Given a corpus of story events categorised into 9 topics, we approximate a deep reinforcement learning agent policy to recombine them in order to satisfy narrative structure. We also propose an evaluation of such a system. The evaluation is based on coherence, interest, and topic, in order to figure how much sense the generated stories make, how interesting they are, and examine whether new narrative topics can emerge.

1 Introduction

In this work reinforcement learning is used in conjunction with a shallow generative artificial neural network (ANN) to generate novel stories. First, a SkipGram (Mikolov et al., 2013) based model is derived that generates parts of the narrative in a local neighbourhood (a few consecutive events at time). An artificial agent is then used to extend its use to the whole narrative while globally adhering to the story structure learned by that model.

2 Previous Work

Data-driven approaches for story generation can be found in (McIntyre and Lapata, 2009; Li et al., 2013). In (McIntyre and Lapata, 2009), the authors present an end-to-end system to generate stories by deriving models of interest and coherence and a generator that creates stories by consulting a knowledge base of story elements and their possible interactions. They improved their work in (McIntyre and Lapata, 2010) by generating stories with genetic algorithms instead of specified models for interest. In (Li et al., 2013), the authors recombine events found in a story corpus with a planning algorithm to create novel stories which consist of events in the form of simple sentences. Their novelty relies on that they crowd-source the corpus in natural language sentences and do not need to provide a pre-defined knowledge base. In that work, they use paraphrase identification using weighted dependencies (Lintean and Rus, 2009) in order to group similar events which they use to construct graphs of narration and a planning algorithm to generate new stories. (Riedl and Harrison, 2016) use that work together with Reinforcement Learning in order to teach artificial agents human values. Deep Reinforcement Learning has been explored in the context of natural language generation before in the context of text-based games. In (Narasimhan et al., 2015) the authors introduce a recurrent neural network which they call LSTM-DQN, to characterise the states of the worlds of text-based Multi-User Dungeon games. They then use Deep Q-learning (Mnih and others, 2015) to learn optimal policies for such games. In (He et al., 2016) the authors introduce a novel type of ANN called Deep Reinforcement Relevance Network which allows for separate ANNs to use for the states and actions of the agents allowing actions of arbitrary number or complexity to be taken by the agent. In this work we use such a network with an actor-critic method and devise a

*Correspondence should be sent to the first author. This paper has been sponsored by RPPtv Ltd.

Proceedings of the INLG 2017 Workshop on Computational Creativity and Natural Language Generation, pages 38–43,
Santiago de Compostela, September 2017.

data driven approach for story generation to learn how to construct narratives from a collection of stories.

3 Methodology

3.1 Event Representation

We used 519 stories from the SCHEHERAZADE system (Li et al., 2013)[1] which contains simple stories pertaining to 9 topics with an average length of 7-16 events per story per topic. These stories consist of simple sentences, each describing a single event. Using the Stanford NLP parser, we extract the Universal Dependencies (Chen and Manning, 2014; Nivre et al., 2016) of each sentence as a list of relations in the form $rel(head, modifier)$ where rel is the relation type and $head$, $modifier$ are literals. We further lemmatize each $head$ and $modifier$ using WordNet (Miller, 1995) in order to reduce the total number of literals we have to deal with. Narratives are sequences of events which in turn are simple sentences that describe a character action or a stative. We use universal dependencies and a shallow ANN in order to derive a useful and compact representation for each event. Having derived a set of all the dependencies found in the corpus each event is represented as a vector $\boldsymbol{v}_k$ of the form $[H_{dep1}\ H_{dep2}\ \ldots M_{dep1}\ M_{dep2}]^T$ where H_{dep} corresponds to the head of dependency dep, M_{dep} to the modifier and each of those elements can take as values an integer that serves as the index for the literals found in the corpus.

After we extract a vector $\boldsymbol{v}_k$ for each event k in our corpus, we use an ANN to learn a compact representation of our events such that two similar events have similar representations. Instead of measuring grammatical similarity as in (Li et al., 2013) we consider as similar events the ones that are used in a similar context. For this we use a model similar to the SkipGram (Mikolov et al., 2013). This model derives a low-dimensional fixed-length representation space that maps events that are used similarly, close in that space thus implicitly "grouping" them together. It also gives probabilities of each event happening, based on previous events. The SkipGram model can be seen in Figure 1a.

[1] http://boyangli.co/openstory.php

Choosing such a model allows us to capture relations between neighbouring events, in a similar way to that of the original SkipGram that captures analogies of words in language. We can then use these learned relations to generate events that satisfy them and thus create "coherent" narratives. It also allows us to implicitly group events. This means that, in the process of generating a narrative, when choosing on an event to include, we do have a probability of including a different, but similar, event. Finally, we can use it with events not found in the corpus it has been trained with. As long as we can feed it a vector representation of the new event it will be mapped close to similar events in the corpus. We will see that by using the model generatively to predict the context from a starting event we can already make sensible narratives.

3.2 Generative Model

In Section 3.1 we introduced our SkipGram Model. This model has been trained to give an approximation of the context of an event, given that event. The context of an event in our case consists of the events that immediately surround it. By starting from a random event that can begin a narrative, the model gives the probability of the next event. An example of a narrative generated can be seen in Figure 2b. Generating narratives this way, while it appears adequate, suffers from a serious limitation. Since the model is trained on an event and its immediate surroundings, it is not possible to capture longer distance dependencies in the narrative. In other words, we cannot interrupt a coherent sequence of events and come at it later so the model is "forced" to keep very close to the corpus in order to maintain coherence.

3.3 Deep Reinforcement Learning

Reinforcement learning is the field that studies how an abstract mathematical entity, called an *agent*, can interact with an environment $\mathcal{E}$ in order to maximise a numerical quantity (Sutton and Barto, 1998). We call an instance of the environment at time t a *state* s_t, the quantity to maximise a *utility* U_t. The agent interacts with the environment by executing a series of *actions* a_i and receiving a series of immediate *rewards* r_t. The utility U_t is related to the immediate rewards r_t by the expression: $U_t = \sum_{n=1}^{t} r_n$. The series of actions the agent takes based on the

Proceedings of the INLG 2017 Workshop on Computational Creativity and Natural Language Generation, pages 38–43,
Santiago de Compostela, September 2017.

state of the environment is modelled by a *policy* π. The policy can be seen as a probability distribution $\pi(a_t = a_i|s_t)$. The problem of reinforcement learning therefore is to find a policy that maximises the utility for the agent in a given environment. In order to generate policies, RL algorithms usually approximate a *value function* $V(s_t)$ or an *action-value function* $Q(s_t, a_t)$. $V(s_t)$ gives a measure of how beneficial is for the agent to exist at the state s_t and $Q(s_t, a_t)$ how beneficial it is for the agent to be at state s_t and execute action a_t. Deep Reinforcement Learning (DRL) approximates Q, V, $\mathcal{E}$, or π with a Deep Neural Network. A popular approach for training agents works by suggesting an action a_t using a model called an *actor* and evaluates it using a model called a *critic*. The method we use in this work is called Deep Deterministic Policy Gradient (Lillicrap et al., 2016) with the actor and critic models being the deep neural networks that appear in Figures 1b and 1c respectively. The model of the critic is inspired by the Deep Reinforcement Relevance Network given in (He et al., 2016). The actor approximates an event to be included in the narrative and the critic evaluates it based on the current state of the narrative. The state of the narrative is at every point a simple concatenation of the embeddings (as given by the hidden layer in 1a) of the events included in that narrative until that point. At every step the reward is calculated based on the distance of the expected action-event to the selected event so that it awards adding events to the narrative when those are close to the ones we expect to see, and punishes by a small amount unexpected events. Punishing unexpected events might appear counter-intuitive at first glance since story generation systems are expected to generate unexpected events. This is compensated by the stochastic nature of policies found by actor-critic methods which will also assign a small probability to an unexpected event happening.

4 Evaluation

In order to evaluate the system's capability to generate interesting narratives human evaluation is necessary. Towards this goal, an evaluation experiment has been designed which is based on similar evaluation approaches found in data-driven story generation approaches (Li et al., 2013; McIntyre and Lapata, 2010) and asks 20 subjects to evaluate 40 narratives from which 10 are from our corpus of human-made narratives, 10 narratives generated by randomly combining events from the corpus, 10 are narratives generated by the SkipGram Model given in Figure 1a and 10 by the DDPG agent. Each subject evaluates 8 narratives based on number of edits (rearranging, deleting, or adding new events) required to make the narrative more coherent, interest rated on a scale from 1 to 5 (1 being "Not at all interesting" and 5 being "Very Interesting") as well as asked to give one word that better describes the topic of the narrative. This last task can helps us figure out whether new topics emerge from our system by combining events from different topics. Since this is work in progress, we lack experiment results. In the absence of human evaluation results we could do some qualitative examining of generated narratives. Figures 2a and 2c show narratives found in our original corpus and in Figures 2b and 2d narratives generated by the generative model and the DDPG agent respectively. We can see that the narrative in 2b tries to follow the narrative found in 2c however it deviates in its conclusion. Instead of kneeling in front of Sally and proposing, the narrative ends with John kissing Sally. An important note here is that for the most first part of the narrative, the generative model followed almost exactly the story found in the corpus. This is a weakness of the model that arises from learning relations only between neighbouring events. A more interesting narrative is the one found in 2d. This narrative combines events from the narrative in Figure 2a, the one in 2c, as well as others found in the corpus. Narratives generated by the DDPG agent tend to explore more events while narratives generated by the generative model tend to stick to the corpus.

5 Discussion/Future Work

We have presented a system that can learn narrative structure from a collection of stories presented in natural language. This work builds on the work of (Li et al., 2013) and tries to improve it in several ways. First, instead of grouping events based on grammatical similarity we use similarity based on context. In that work, events are also parsed into universal dependencies and grammatical similarity

Proceedings of the INLG 2017 Workshop on Computational Creativity and Natural Language Generation, pages 38–43, Santiago de Compostela, September 2017. ©2017 Association for Computational Linguistics

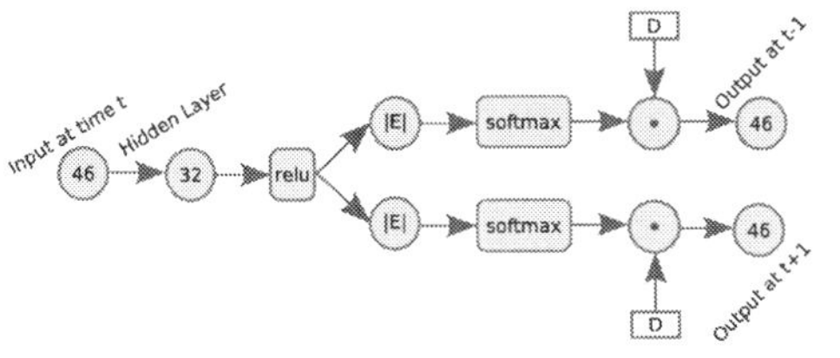

(a) SkipGram model

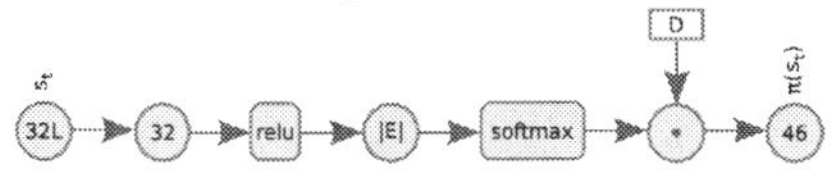

(b) actor

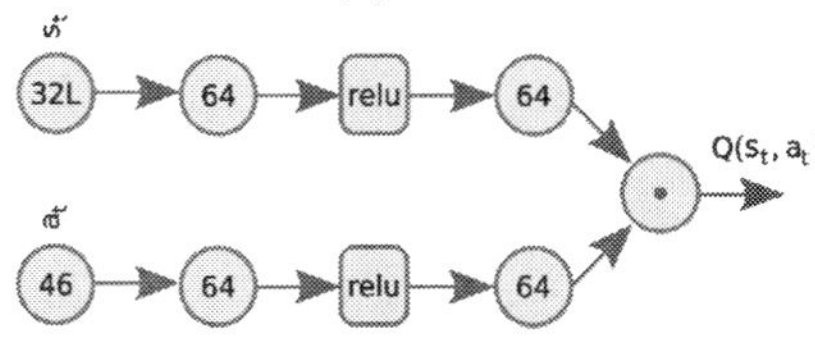

(c) critic

Figure 1: The Skipgram model, and the models for the actor and the critic. Circles represent fully connected neuron layers with the number of neurons being the number inside the circle. The smoothed rectangles represent the activation functions with `relu` being the linear rectifier and `softmax` a softmax output. $|E|$ is the number of events in our database, and D the narrative corpus as a matrix of features. The dot symbolises the dot product. L is the number of the events making up the narrative, $\pi(s_t)$ the policy at state s_t, $Q(s_t, a_t)$ the state-action value for the policy π.

" *John loved Sally John wanted to marry Sally John bought an engagement ring John took Sally to the park John and Sally enjoyed a picnic John got down on one knee John presented the ring to Sally Sally started to cry John asked Sally to marry John Sally agreed Sally put on the ring John and Sally hugged* "

(a) An example narrative from the corpus.

" *John entered Sally's house. John and Sally entered the living room. John and Sally sat on the sofa. John picked up Sally's hand. John kissed Sally's hand. Sally smiled at John. John let go of Sally's hand. John stood up. John kissed Sally.* "

(b) An example narrative generated by using the SkipGram Model generatively.

" *Sally opened the door. John entered Sally's house. John and Sally entered the living room. John and Sally sat on the sofa. John picked up Sally's hand. John kissed Sally's hand. Sally smiled at John. John let go of Sally's hand. John stood up. John kneeled in front of Sally. John took a ring box out of his pocket. Sally pressed both hands against her cheeks. John proposed to Sally. Sally took the ring box from John. Sally opened the ring box. Sally took the ring out of the ring box. John took the ring from Sally. John put the ring on Sally's left third finger.* "

(c) An example narrative from the corpus.

" *John loved Sally. John presented the ring to Sally. John let go of Sally's hand. Sally and John laughed. Sally and John kissed. John told Sally how beautiful she is. Sally blushed.* "

(d) An example narrative generated by using the DDPG agent.

Figure 2: Examples of narratives.

between the heads and modifiers of the same dependencies is used to cluster events. This requires similar sentence structure for different events in order for such similarity to be meaningful. We get past this limitation by deriving a fixed length representation by using the model in Figure 1a and thus we are able to compare sentences of variable structure. Since our similarity is based on how events are used in a narrative, we can interchangeably use two sentences that refer to the same event but are grammatically different (e.g. "Sally agreed to marry John." and "Sally said yes.").

The second is that the use of an agent allows for complex relations in the narrative, unknown in advance, to be captured as showcased by (Narasimhan et al., 2015; He et al., 2016), as well as arbitrary authorial goals when carefully introduced in the reward function. One could for example augment the corpus of available events with information about emotions (Francisco and Hervás, 2007) and then reward events with the desired emotional content. The use of an agent that can also create narrative allows usage in a multiagent, or even interactive environment. This is not very obvious in the current work because experiments have not been yet conducted but an example would be an agent that learned from narratives of topic "proposal", another that learned from "affairs" to work together (i.e. by alternating between the choices of the two agents after a couple of sentences), to produce something in the lines of a "family drama".

Proceedings of the INLG 2017 Workshop on Computational Creativity and Natural Language Generation, pages 38–43, Santiago de Compostela, September 2017. ©2017 Association for Computational Linguistics

The current research leaves some things to be desired. While he have designed an experiment for the evaluation of the system, we have yet to run it through human subjects, who are the ones who can judge if a system exhibits creativity. We cannot therefore have a discussion about whether our system is creative. The narrative generation capacity is limited among other things by the corpus itself. We can only make as many novel stories as can be made by recombining the available events. Given that the vectors of the events (Section 3.1) in the corpus constitute only a limited subset of values in that vector space we should be able to generate novel events mapped from within that space once we had a way to map from narrative to surface text. In (Kumagai et al., 2016), the authors present a system that can generate language given syntactic structure as well as semantic information. Our event vector representation maintains syntactic structure data which could be combined with that work to generate surface text. Another issue is that learning is done exclusively on the narrative-structure level without taking into account any consideration any extra information in the stories. One could use characterisation of story events and heuristics of narration similar to the *STellA* system presented in (León and Gervás, 2014). We speculate that such heuristics can be used as rewards in the context of reinforcement learning and thus guide learning. More technical issues relate to problems that can be met both in reinforcement and in deep learning. Training the networks and the agent is sensitive to hyper-parameters as well as network architecture. Since this is work in progress both the architecture and the hyperparameters have been chosen intuitively by hand and by no means we can claim these are optimal. Better design parameters can be chosen in a robust way through exhaustive cross validation.

References

Danqi Chen and Christopher Manning. 2014. A Fast and Accurate Dependency Parser using Neural Networks. In *Proceedings of the 2014 Conference on Empirical Methods in Natural Language Processing*, EMNLP 2014, pages 740–750. ACL.

Virginia Francisco and Raquel Hervás. 2007. Emotag: Automated mark up of affective information in texts. In *Proceedings of Doctoral Consortium at the 8th EUROLAN summer school*, pages 5–12.

Ji He, Jianshu Chen, Xiaodong He, Jianfeng Gao, Lihong Li, Li Deng, and Mari Ostendorf. 2016. Deep Reinforcement Learning with a Natural Language Action Space. In *Proceedings of the 54th Annual Meeting of the Association for Computational Linguistics*, pages 1621–1630. ACL.

Kaori Kumagai, Ichiro Kobayashi, Daichi Mochihashi, Hideki Asoh, Tomoaki Nakamura, and Takayuki Nagai. 2016. Human-like Natural Language Generation Using Monte Carlo Tree Search. In *The INLG 2016 Workshop on Computational Creativity in Natural Language Generation*, pages 11–18. ACL.

Carlos León and Pablo Gervás. 2014. Creativity in story generation from the ground up: Nondeterministic simulation driven by narrative. In *Proceedings of the 5th International Conference on Computational Creativity*, ICCC 2014.

B. Li, , S. Lee-Urban, , G. Johnston, and M. O. Riedl. 2013. Story Generation with Crowdsourced Plot Graphs. In *Proceedings of the Twenty-Seventh AAAI Conference on Artificial Intelligence*, pages 598–604. AAAI Press.

Timothy Paul Lillicrap, Jonathan James Hunt, Alexander Pritzel, Nicolas Manfred Otto Heess, Tom Erez, Yuval Tassa, David Silver, and Daniel Pieter Wierstra. 2016. Continuous control with deep reinforcement learning. In *Proceedings of 4th International Conference on Learning Representations*, ICLR 2016.

Mihai Lintean and Vasile Rus. 2009. Paraphrase identification using weighted dependencies and word semantics. In *Proceedings of the Twenty-Second International Florida Artificial Intelligence Research Society Conference*, FLAIRS 2009. AAAI Press.

Neil McIntyre and Mirella Lapata. 2009. Learning to tell tales: A data-driven approach to story generation. In *Proceedings of the Joint Conference of the 47th Annual Meeting of the ACL and the 4th International Joint Conference on Natural Language Processing of the AFNLP*, pages 217–225. ACL.

Neil McIntyre and Mirella Lapata. 2010. Plot induction and evolutionary search for story generation. In *Proceedings of the 48th Annual Meeting of the Association for Computational Linguistics*, pages 1562–1572. ACL.

Tomas Mikolov, Kai Chen, Greg Corrado, and Jeffrey Dean. 2013. Efficient estimation of word representations in vector space. In *ArXiv e-prints*, volume abs/1301.3781.

G. A. Miller. 1995. WordNet: A Lexical Database for English. *Communications of the ACM*, 38(11).

Proceedings of the INLG 2017 Workshop on Computational Creativity and Natural Language Generation, pages 38–43,
Santiago de Compostela, September 2017.

Volodymyr Mnih and others. 2015. Human-level control through deep reinforcement learning. *Nature*, 518(7540):529–533.

Karthik Narasimhan, Tejas Kulkarni, and Regina Barzilay. 2015. Language understanding for text-based games using deep reinforcement learning. In *Proceedings of the 2015 Conference on Empirical Methods in Natural Language Processing*, pages 1–11. ACL.

Joakim Nivre, Marie-Catherine de Marneffe, Filip Ginter, Yoav Goldberg, Jan Hajic, Christopher D. Manning, Ryan McDonald, Slav Petrov, Sampo Pyysalo, Natalia Silveira, Reut Tsarfaty, and Daniel Zeman. 2016. Universal dependencies v1: A multilingual treebank collection. In *Proceedings of the Tenth International Conference on Language Resources and Evaluation*, LREC 2016. ELRA.

Mark O Riedl and Brent Harrison. 2016. Using stories to teach human values to artificial agents. In *Papers from the 2016 AAAI Workshop on AI, Ethics, and Society*. AAAI Press.

Richard S. Sutton and Andrew G. Barto. 1998. *Introduction to Reinforcement Learning*, volume 135. MIT Press, 1st edition.

Proceedings of the INLG 2017 Workshop on Computational Creativity and Natural Language Generation, pages 38–43,
Santiago de Compostela, September 2017.

Association for Computational Linguistics
209 N. Eighth Street
Stroudsburg, Pennsylvania 18360

ISBN 978-1-5108-4760-6

CURRAN ASSOCIATES INC.
proceedings.com